C000260038

Succ
Coars
and Methods

Angling 1672

Angling 1972 (*Alfred Pond*)

Successful Angling

Coarse Fishing Tackle and Methods

Richard Walker
Fred J. Taylor
Fred Buller
Hugh Falkus

Stanley Paul
London Melbourne Auckland Johannesburg

Stanley Paul & Co. Ltd

An imprint of Century Hutchinson Ltd

Brookmount House, 62 – 65 Chandos Place,
Covent Garden, London WC2N 4NW

Century Hutchinson Australia (Pty) Ltd
PO Box 496, 16 – 22 Church Street, Hawthorn, Melbourne, Victoria 3122

Century Hutchinson New Zealand Limited
32 – 34 View Road, PO Box 40 – 086, Glenfield, Auckland 10

Century Hutchinson South Africa (Pty) Ltd
PO Box 337, Bergvlei 2012, South Africa

First published 1977
Reprinted 1979, 1981, 1983, 1984, 1987

Printed and bound in Great Britain by
Anchor Brendon Ltd, Tiptree, Essex

ISBN 0 09 129281 6

Contents

The Trotter; The Shot-dragger; The Ducker; The Wire Avon; Laying-on; Stret-pegging; Aspects of Lift-fishing; The Windbeater; The Zoomer; The Cocktail.

Introduction

As Patrick Chalmers said, only non-angling snobs ever considered 'coarse' fishing to be inferior to game fishing: 'The man who invented the term had the soul of a lackey.'

Chalmers was a true sportsman. He saw no need to differentiate between fish with adipose fins and those without. It is unfortunate that the term 'coarse' is still in use, and likely to remain so, but today more and more anglers accept the fact that there is no difference in sporting value between game fish and so-called 'coarse' fish. The dividing wall between the species is slowly being demolished. And why not? It never existed in the days of Walton, Venables, Pennell, Bickerdyke and Sheringham – to name but a few in the list of famous angling authors. They pursued every kind of fish with equal enthusiasm and interest.

Some of the best reservoir-trout anglers started off on coarse fish and later applied their skill and knowledge to game fishing, and a great number of confirmed game fishermen have, over the years, reached the conclusion that there is nothing coarse about 'coarse' fishing. Indeed, they have extended their season to such an extent that they now fish for twelve months of the year instead of five or six – and, which is more, they are enjoying it. That, after all, is what the sport of fishing is about.

However, coarse fishing is all the more enjoyable if it is approached in the right way. During the last twenty years an outstanding aspect of the sport has been what may be called the 'scientific' approach. This is not so much a matter of new discoveries as the more general application of scientific knowledge to the manufacture of tackle and to the various ways of using it. This little book, based on the results of modern research, is aimed at guiding the angler in his choice of tackle and angling methods. Helping him to understand why, where, when and how certain materials and methods should be preferred will, we hope, help him to think things out for himself.

RICHARD WALKER, FRED J. TAYLOR, FRED BULLER, HUGH FALKUS

Fred Taylor fishing for carp at Bierton

1 The Approach

It is sometimes said that to become a successful coarse fisherman it is necessary to think like a fish. But that is probably asking too much – even if such a thing were possible. However it is essential in angling, as it is in the hunting of all wild creatures to consider the *senses* of the quarry we pursue; to realize that fish can see and smell and hear. This is perhaps the most important factor involved in the pursuit of coarse fish. The trout angler knows it well. And he applies it to his fishing simply because he is often able to see a fish before he attempts to catch it. He has learned that fish are sensitive to vibrations caused by heavy-footed humans. He has also learned that if he can see the trout, the trout can sometimes see him and if it does so his chances of catching it are nil!

As long ago as 1836, Alfred Ronalds explained in his *Fly Fisherman's Entomology* that light is refracted when it passes from air to water and vice versa, and that this has an important bearing on what a fish can see above the surface of the water, If, for example, the top of an angler's hat is 6 feet above the surface, a fish within 23 yards can see it. If the fish is farther away than 23 yards, it can see nothing of the angler. The relationship is linear: if the height of the angler above the water's surface is reduced, the fish has to be proportionately nearer before he sees the top of the angler's head or hat. If that is only 3 feet above the water's surface, then the fish has to be as near as $11\frac{1}{2}$ yards before the angler is in sight.

The fish sees the outside world through a transparent or translucent circle above its head; beyond the circumference of this circle the surface appears to the fish as a mirror in which the underwater landscape is reflected. Therefore, all the light that reaches the fish must pass through the circle above it. Consequently the fish can easily detect any interruption in the light. If the angler moves into a position where he causes such an interruption, the fish will know it

R.W. uses stealth, caution
and concealment to
approach a clear-water
roach swim on the River
Kennett

Unlike R.W. this angler
shows no regard for
concealement and is
therefore in full view of the
fish

even if the water is muddy or stained. If it is sufficiently clear to allow any light to reach the fish, then the fish can perceive an interruption of the light and may take fright as a result.

These facts, made known more than a century ago, have been elaborated frequently since, but mainly in fly-fishing literature. It is only recently that coarse-fish anglers have become aware of them and understood the importance of concealment and camouflage. The following rules apply to all forms of fishing:

1. Keep as low as possible while fishing.
2. Avoid being silhouetted against the skyline.
3. Wear clothes (especially hats) that blend with the colours of the banks and bankside vegetation.
4. Avoid flash caused by ultra-glossy rods and other items of equipment.

These rules should not be relaxed even when the water is muddy or stained, or the surface broken by ripple or waves. In such circumstances the fish cannot see the angler clearly, but, unless he behaves circumspectly, they can tell that he is there. The fact that the water is murky and the fish cannot be seen by the angler does not mean that the angler, when high up on the bank, cannot be seen by the fish. On the contrary, he is very much in view and any sudden movement on the bank will make them cautious, if only for a short time.

Sometimes it is not possible to reach the water's edge without causing a disturbance, but when it is practicable, a 'redskin' approach will always improve the chance of success. Where it is impossible to approach the bank without disturbance, it is better by far to make that disturbance at once and have done with it before settling down, concealed and comfortable, to wait until the fish (which will undoubtedly have been scared) return to the swim.

Have everything to hand once you are settled so that unnecessary movements are eliminated. At all times *keep below the skyline and try to blend with the bankside surroundings. Then* the fish will come back. At times they may need the encouragement of a little groundbait or free samples of hookbait, but whatever is offered should be done discreetly and with as little disturbance as possible.

It is not generally recognized that at times some species of coarse fish can be caught if the angler employs the trout fisherman's careful 'hands and knees' approach. Chub and carp, for instance, are often

Although, when photographed, Louie Thompson of Sheffield literally had her feet in the water, her drab clothing and her closeness to the water helped her merge with a background of high bank and vegetation. She was ideally positioned to ledger for this 6 lb chub, hooked on cheese paste 15 yards downstream

to be seen browsing near the surface on hot summer days and can be caught with the simplest of tackle. But the skill lies in being able to reach the fish without being seen yourself.

It doesn't always work, but there is more than an even chance that if you can drop a lobworm, slug, crayfish, or any one of a dozen different natural baits within the 'window' of a chub's vision, it will be taken without any preliminaries whatever. Very often a bait dropped immediately *behind* a chub will cause it to swirl and take – and to be hooked before it realizes its mistake. That is exciting fishing. It is fishing which can be selective too, because it is often possible to choose between a small chub and one of considerably larger proportions. The fact that the smaller of the two is often the faster moving and, despite your efforts to prevent it from doing so, still manages to beat the bigger fish to the bait, is all part of the game and adds to the excitement.

It is not always possible to apply the same procedure to carp. They can be seen, and they can be caught by stealth and cunning, but they must be given time. The bait, a piece of floating crust, is cast from concealment into the *general area* and not directly to the fish itself. Somehow a carp manages to detect the presence of bread on the water. Perhaps the 'flavour' permeates or the bait is spotted from some distance away. Whatever the reason for the carp's interest, it is an exciting moment when the investigation starts. The great fish swims up to the hooked piece of crust, eyes it, noses it, swirls at it, turns away, returns, inspects it again and after perhaps half an hour of nail-biting tension opens its mouth and sucks it in. That, or the fish knocks it off the hook and devours the pieces on their way down!

When you are faced with these situations, and sit hardly daring to breathe in case you alarm the fish, you realize the importance of making the full use of cover. You appreciate the fact that in this respect fish are no different from rabbits, foxes or other wild animals. You would not expect a rabbit to stay where it was long enough for you to catch it if you walked up to it in full view. Nor should you expect a fish to do so.

There are many other considerations, of course, and the question of baits, tackle, time of day, location, weather conditions and a host of other factors must be taken in account. But it is vital to remember that the best tackle, the best baits, the best times and the best conditions will be useless if you do not take the simple precaution of approaching silently and unseen. The best tackle in the world will not catch you a fish that isn't there!

'Secrets' of success

During the many years that R.W. and F.J.T. have spent writing regular columns for the angling press hundreds of letters have been received from readers asking for the 'secrets' of their success. Some readers, it seems, imagine that there is a secret essence which can be mixed with various baits to make them (as the readers put it) 'irresistible to fish'! There is, of course, no such essence. Too many anglers want a short cut to success. They will accept advice involving complex tackles and methods, or exotic baits, but reject advice about simple things that really make the difference between success and failure. There are five simple but important precepts:

1. *Find where the fish are*

There is a saying in the Army: 'Time spent in reconnaissance is seldom wasted.' In fishing, it is *never* wasted. It is better to spend six hours finding the best place to fish and two hours fishing it successfully than eight hours catching nothing from the wrong swim or pitch. There are many ways in which the presence of fish can be detected; they may roll on the surface, or leap, or send up bubbles, or stir up mud, or cause small fry to leap or scatter. If the water is clear enough, you may be able to see the fish themselves. Failing any such signs, remember Surtees's famous character Facey Romford, who said: 'Francis Romford, moy beloved friend, if you were a fox, where would you choose to lie?' Substitute fish for fox, and you have it.

Fish are not concerned with your comfort, only their own. If your idea of a good swim is a place where you can sit comfortably, with the wind behind you, no weeds nearby, no branches to entangle your tackle, and so on, you will not succeed often. First you must locate the fish; secondly, overcome the difficulties entailed in fishing for them.

2. *Having found the fish, don't scare them*

A well-known angler, when a little boy, was told by his grandfather always to pretend that the fish he was after had a gun and would shoot him if it could. That advice serves well. Next to not fishing where the fish are, the commonest cause of failure is that the angler has scared his quarry.

'Fish are not concerned with your comfort, only their own' (see text). Here F.J.T. has chosen his position mindful of this truism

Fish can see you. They can also detect vibrations caused by a heavy footfall on the bank. Splashy casting, the glint of your rod, line or float may also scare them. True, they may return after being scared, but it is much better to avoid scaring them in the first place. Even when a fish has been hooked, it still pays to avoid scaring it. A big fish can often be brought to the net on the finest tackle if it never sees the angler.

3. *Fish at the right time*

The right time to fish is when the fish are willing to feed, and that means you must suit your fishing times to theirs, not expect them to change their habits so that you can catch them. Many factors affect the feeding times of fish and if you want to succeed you must learn about them. In summer and early autumn, early morning and late evening are usually the best times; in winter, if the weather is cold, you usually do best around midday, but if it is mild, late evening is often productive. On some waters, early and late fishing, or fishing at night, are essential to avoid boat traffic and other disturbances.

Hundreds of thousands of anglers fish at the wrong time in places where there are great numbers of good fish – which could be caught if their feeding times were studied.

4. *Use the right tackle*

Your outfit must be capable of placing the bait where the fish can find it, preferably with the least possible disturbance; of detecting bites when they come; of driving the hook home, and of exercising enough control over a hooked fish to keep it clear of weeds and snags until it is sufficiently tired to be led to the net. Most anglers are well aware of this but fail to put into practice what they know because of mistaken ideas about angling ethics, involving the belief that it is more creditable to fish with inadequate than with adequate tackle.

It is not sportsmanlike to use tackle so light that if you hook a big fish you are likely to be broken. Fish that have been hooked and lost are as hard to catch as those that have been landed and returned. If they are left trailing a length of line they are almost impossible to catch until they get rid of it and then it is left in the water to entangle some unfortunate bird. So use the strongest tackle and the biggest hooks that the fish will take. If you use tackle that is too coarse, you'll get no bites, so tackle strength has always to strike a compromise. But if you have located your fish, avoided scaring them, and chosen to fish at a time when they are feeding, you can usually tempt them to bite on tackle strong enough to land them, provided you make no mistakes in your handling.

5. *Choose the right bait*

The choice of baits in coarse-fish angling is enormous. Nowadays, most of Britain's coarse-fish anglers are so lazy that the only baits they ever think of using are maggots and chrysalids (or casters). These baits are useful at times, albeit very expensive, but more often other, cheaper baits, are far more effective, especially when you are after bigger fish. Remember that you can often discriminate against unwanted small fish by using baits of comparatively large size.

Remember also that although fish are not possessed of high intelligence, they are capable of learning by experience and that on heavily fished waters a high proportion of the fish have been caught and returned at some stage of their lives. Many fish have suffered the experience several times and have learned to avoid certain baits.

The enterprising angler, by offering them alternatives, can often succeed where more conservative fishermen fail. Generally speaking, the bigger the fish, the more likely they are to have learned, and thus the greater the need for the angler to seek not only different baits but different ways of presenting those baits that fall outside the experience of the big crafty fish he wants to catch.

These, then, are the essentials for success that no angler who wishes to succeed can afford to neglect:

Find where the fish are
Having found the fish, don't scare them
Fish at the right time
Use the right tackle
Choose the right bait

Perhaps we should add a sixth: *take care of your tackle.* Make good, safe knots and test them. Test your hooks for sharpness and correct temper. Keep them sharp. Examine the rings of your rods for grooving. Check that the strength of your line hasn't deteriorated. Keep your reels clean and lubricated. Make sure that coils of line aren't crossed and trapped on the spool or drum of the reel.

In other words, watch all the tiny details. A very small thing can lose you the fish of a lifetime or make all the difference between tempting a big fish to bite and failing to do so. We often hear an angler say: 'Oh, I don't think *that*' (referring to some tiny detail like the colour of a float body, or the choice of a knot) 'could make any difference!' Well, maybe it can't; but if you take the view that any little thing that could possibly improve your angling effectiveness, and couldn't in any way decrease it, ought to be used, you'll find that all those little details of improvement can add up to a considerable overall gain.

Success in angling is not due to luck. The late A. E. Hobbs, one of the greatest anglers who ever lived, said rightly that although luck played a great part in angling, over the years the bad and the good luck balanced out, and what remained was what an angler deserved.

There are no easy roads to success, nor will luck aid the incompetent angler often enough for his satisfaction. Angling is the most complex of all sports; nobody ever lives long enough to learn more than a little about it, though knowledge *can* be gained in large measures by reading as well as by practical experience.

Those who say you can learn more in an hour at the waterside than from all the books and articles ever written are fools. Practical experience is, of course, essential, but the sensible angler reinforces his experience with the wisdom distilled from centuries of angling – which he can find in most public libraries.

Ultimately his success as an angler will depend on his own knowledge, skill, judgement, perseverance and enthusiasm. To continue to believe in 'secret essences' and nonsense of that sort will merely prolong his feeling of frustration and dissatisfaction.

The influence of the weather

Here ye shall wyte in what weder ye shall angle, as I sayd before ina derke lowrynge daye whanne the wynde blowyth softly. And in somer season whan it is brennynge hote thenne it is nought. From Septembre unto Apryll in a fayr sonny daye is ryght good to angle. And yf the wynde in that season have any parte of the Oryent: the wedyr thenne is nought. And whan it is a grete wynde. And whan it snowith reynyth or hayllyth, or is a grete tempeste as thondyr or lightenynge: or a swoly hote weder: thenne it is noughte for to angle.

Dame Juliana Berners, *A Treatyse of Fysshynge wyth an Angle* (1496)

For centuries the weather has provided an ever-ready and plausible excuse for angling failure. This has been (and still is) a comfort to the unsuccessful angler – whose reasons for a blank day are legion: the fish were off the feed because the water was too high or too low; it was too hot or too cold; there was thunder, fog, bright sunshine, moonlight, snow, wind or heavy rain. And so on.

He has a point. It is likely that a good deal of fluctuation in the behaviour of fishes is due to fluctuation in their oxygen supply, and since that supply is affected by weather conditions, the weather can be said to affect the behaviour of fish. Nevertheless, failure to catch fish is more likely to be due to an angler's incompetence than to the weather alone. Or perhaps it would be kinder to say to his inability to make a correct assessment of how the prevailing weather conditions were affecting the fish, and to adjust his tackle and method accordingly.

A fish cannot live without oxygen. It depends on a constant supply of oxygen just as we do, although, since it lives in water, it gets it in a different way. It respires by drawing water into the mouth and expelling it through the gills. The blood vessels in the gill filaments absorb the oxygen which is dissolved in the water, in return for carbon dioxide and other waste products. The oxygen is then distributed throughout the fish's body.

The amount of dissolved oxygen available to a fish varies from a number of different causes, including wind, rain, broken water (ripple, rapids, waterfalls), temperature, water pollution and, to a small extent, atmospheric pressure.

The effect of pollution is to reduce the oxygen content of the water until, in extreme cases, the water becomes unfit for any form of aquatic life. Unfortunately, there are many examples of this.

By comparison, changes in atmospheric pressure have very little effect on fish. An increase in pressure certainly causes more oxygen to dissolve. When the pressure decreases, oxygen tends to be driven off. But the variation in the amount of dissolved oxygen is small compared with the effects of temperature change, rapids, waterfalls, ripple, rain and wind.

The effect of wind is to increase dissolved oxygen by disturbing the surface and, usually, by reducing water temperature. Cold water is capable of containing more dissolved oxygen than warm water. As the water temperature rises, so oxygenation decreases.

Rain has a similar effect to wind. But in areas where the level of air pollution is very high, rain may temporarily increase the acidity of the water to the extent that fish cease to feed. Rainwater draining off the land may not only discolour a river but carry various chemicals in the form of pesticides, herbicides and fertilizers whose effect upon fish can vary from slightly sickening to lethal.

The effect of discoloration varies from one river or lake to another. Only a small increase in colour will inhibit fish from feeding in what are normally clear chalk-streams; whereas in many rain-fed rivers a similar increase in colour will start fish feeding eagerly. In lakes fish often congregate where an in-flowing stream is discharging stained or muddy water.

Sunshine raises water temperature, and so has the effect of decreasing oxygenation. But if there is a large amount of weed in the water, photosynthesis will more than overcome this effect. Thus, owing to the photosynthetic reaction in chlorophyll-bearing aquatic plants, induced by sunlight, these plants assist water to become oxygenated by day. At night, however, they absorb oxygen from the water in return for carbon dioxide.

Decaying vegetation in the water also reduces the oxygen content.

For as long as we can remember, knowledgeable anglers fishing the famous Tring reservoirs of Marsworth, Wilstone and Startops have fished 'into the wind' whenever possible. In the late 1930s when Mr Bench caught these and other great fish few anglers could have known how a lack of oxygen sometimes made the opposite shore fishless

Above: The sometime British record bream (12 lb 15 oz) caught by Mr F. Bench at Tring
Below: Three of Tring's mighty bream — including the record-breaker

Fish certainly seem able to anticipate weather change. They are reluctant to feed when a thunderstorm is brewing, but will start feeding as soon as the storm breaks and the rain begins to fall. When for no obvious reason fish refuse to feed, a change of weather can be expected within twenty-four hours.

In general, settled weather provides the best sport. Fish are put off by sudden changes. But if conditions remain constant for several days fish begin to feed again, even though the conditions may involve very high or low temperatures. In extremes of temperature, however, it pays the angler to seek areas where certain influences tend to alleviate the conditions: a warm spring in very cold weather; a waterfall or rapids when the weather is very hot.

When the air temperature is higher than the water temperature, angling prospects are good. Prospects are poor when the air temperature is lower than the water temperature. But a *rising* air temperature can offer good sport – even though it is still below the water temperature.

With the possible exception of grayling – which seem less affected by changes in water temperature than any other species of fish – a rise in water level caused by melting snow usually deters fish from feeding.

Fish are usually hard to catch when there is bright diffused light from very thin cloud cover. But this is probably due to reasons different from any so far discussed: in such conditions of light, fish are best able to spot every detail of the angler's tackle – and often enough the angler himself!

Good fishing days come in every guise: very cold ones, snowy ones, blustery ones, even very hot ones. Windy days can be an aid to fishing simply because the action of the wind tends to cause confusion to a fish's sense of vision and hearing: waves cause a refractive pitch-and-toss to light beams entering the water and may distract a fish's attention from an angler's movements.

That most famous of pike fishermen, Alfred Jardine, wrote: 'My best sport has been on windy days. . . . The ripples on the surface of the water refract the rays of light, and the angler and his punt are but indifferently seen.' He did not suggest that pike fed voraciously in windy weather; simply that they fed *fearlessly*.

Jardine made another reference to extreme weather conditions when recounting a visit to the River Frome: 'In the main channel thick slabs of ice were hurrying along the swift-flowing current. We fished close to the landlocked ice, and our floats would again and again disappear under the edge of it, as hungered into madness some plunging pike seized our livebaits.'

J. W. Martin ('Trent Otter'), writing in 1907, made an interesting comment on two winter feeding species – pike and roach. On their reactions to similar weather, he said: 'An east wind with a touch of frost that would drive the roach clean off the feed might make a jack come on right manfully.'

The angler who thinks that Martin was correct has an important point to remember: lessons learned about the effects of weather on one species of coarse fish do not *necessarily* apply to other species.

Edward Spence (writing in 1928) discussed the pike's feeding activity during very cold weather. Once, when fishing from a punt on the Royalty Water of the Avon in bitterly cold weather, his punt pole gathered ice to such an extent that he was obliged to tow the punt upriver. Cold slush came down with the stream, and with it went his last chance (so he thought) of catching pike. Yet when, after some hours of fruitless fishing, he changed from livebaiting with float to livebaiting on ledger tackle, he caught eleven pike ranging in size from 5 lb to 11 lb.

On such small details hangs success. Spence's experience indicates that in very cold conditions an anchored bait, lying close to the bed of lake or river, may induce a pike to feed; whereas methods demanding a lot of activity from the fish will not!

Much of what we have written about weather is reflected in the feeding habits of fish. But these will be the subject of the next section.

2 The Fish

Feeding habits

An aspect of coarse-fish angling in which science has played its part concerns the feeding habits of fish. The fact that trout are at times highly selective in their feeding has long been known. This can be seen when there is a heavy hatch of a particular species of insect. If, for example, trout are feeding selectively on Iron Blues, the fly-fisherman knows that he must offer them a reasonable imitation of an Iron Blue if he is to catch any of them.

It is only comparatively recently that it has been realized that this kind of behaviour is common to all kinds of fish and is by no means confined to trout.

Carp and tench often become completely preoccupied with eating bloodworms, the larvae of various species of midge, in the bottom mud. These species, and others, also at times feed selectively on daphnia and other tiny organisms that are subject to periodic population explosions. Roach, and sometimes dace and chub, may be found feeding selectively on silkweed; most members of the carp family indulge in selective feeding on various kinds of water snail when these occur in unusually large numbers.

Perch become preoccupied, sometimes, with eating tiny fish when concentrations of small fry occur in particular areas, and a similar form of behaviour has been noticed in pike.

Unlike the fly fisherman, the coarse fisherman can sometimes turn this facet of fish behaviour to his advantage by groundbaiting. In earlier days, the function of groundbaiting was thought to be simply that of attracting fish into an area which the angler could conveniently fish. It has, however, another and perhaps more important purpose: that of persuading the fish to eat food which the angler can conveniently use as bait.

Maggots, chrysalids, hempseed, stewed wheat, tares and other baits that can be introduced into the chosen area of water in a way that presents the fish with a great many similar food particles are likely to cause the fish to feed selectively and thus increase greatly the angler's chances of success.

Finding out what fish like is another aspect of coarse angling that has been helped by science. Fish feed more freely when their requirements in respect of water temperature and dissolved oxygen are most correctly met. It is known that few fish feed when the water temperature is below 39·2°F (the temperature at which water is heaviest), and that as the temperature falls below about 50°F, the metabolic rate of the fish slows, so that their movements are less active and their food requirements are smaller. In such conditions they are liable to be found wherever the water temperature is above average, as for example, in the vicinity of warm springs, discharges of warmer water, or on temporarily sun-warmed shallows.

Conversely, if water temperature rises above about 70°F, anything that cools the water or otherwise increases its oxygen content, is liable to attract fish and to induce them to feed.

The effect of wind on large areas of deep water is particularly important. The upper layer of water in summer is warmer than that below it and in the absence of wind the depth of this upper layer is approximately uniform in all areas of a lake or reservoir. The effect of wind is to push the upper layer of warmer water to one side of the lake, so that colder water, which is often partly deoxygenated, rises on the windward shore. This is uncongenial to the fish, which move away from it. A thermometer can tell an angler fishing a large water of considerable depth which areas to avoid on any day, and those which he may hopefully fish.

Different species of fish react differently to changes of temperature; grayling, for instance, will feed freely in very cold water where other species would be virtually uncatchable, whereas rudd seem happy in water temperatures high enough to distress most other species. Nevertheless, the knowledge that all kinds of fish are greatly affected by water temperature and dissolved oxygen is of the greatest value to the angler.

Opposite. F.J.T. (top), F.B. (bottom left), R.W. (bottom right) — all seen holding bream over 6¼ lb, taken by them from Wilstone Reservoir

Yet another matter of interest is the reaction by fish to the intensity of the light. A great deal more information is needed before this is properly understood, but it is known that some species of fish exhibit a degree of photophobia and avoid light intensities above a certain level. Tench move into deeper water as the intensity of the light increases; roach start to feed much more actively when the light intensity falls below a certain critical level. Carp, rudd, and chub, on the other hand, seem to enjoy bright sunlight and, if undisturbed, can often be seen basking at the surface.

Arising out of what has already been stated about light refraction, it will be understood that once the sun has fallen below a certain critical angle, which is in fact about 10 degrees to the surface of the water, its direct rays can no longer penetrate, and the only light that does still penetrate will be that reflected from or diffracted by cloud or the earth's atmosphere. Consequently, as the sun sinks, there will be a sharp and sudden reduction in the underwater illumination. The brighter and more cloudless the day, the sharper the reduction will be.

A considerable reduction in underwater illumination makes it almost impossible for surface predators to see the fish, and it seems very likely that the process of evolution has made fish feel safe to forage for food when the direct rays of the sinking sun suddenly cease to penetrate the surface. The evening rise by trout and the tendency of many, if not all, other species of freshwater fish to feed more freely in the late evening may in large measure be due to this sudden reduction in underwater illumination, though doubtless other phenomena are also involved. After a hot day, the cooling-off effect may play a part, and when in the evening the wind drops, as often happens, much greater activity by insects often ensues.

The rapid change in underwater illumination brought about by the change in the sun's angle takes place in reverse in the early morning, and at that time many kinds of fish abandon the shallows and move to deeper water, where they doubtless feel safer.

Anglers who take into account matters of this sort are often accused of being 'too scientific', but the fact is that no scientific training or background is necessary to take advantage of the knowledge science has provided. It is astonishing how an angler who is perfectly willing and able to take his own temperature if he thinks he may have influenza will jib at taking the temperature of the water in which he is fishing, saying that this is 'too scientific', though it may often make all the difference between a good catch and a blank day.

Senses

1. *Vision*

As already stated, the ability of a fish to see above the surface is affected by the refraction of light. This refraction causes a dramatic change in underwater illumination when the angle of the sun to the surface falls below about 10 degrees.

How efficient is the eye of a fish?

It must be remembered that there is a difference between the ability to see, in an optical sense, and the intelligence required to interpret what is seen. If fish had the intelligence to make as good use of their optical equipment as humans can, anglers would seldom have a bite!

2. *Hearing*

The fact that most freshwater fish are able to detect underwater vibrations by means of their lateral lines, and perhaps in other ways as well, is common knowledge, but few people realize how very efficient these vibration detectors are, or over what distances they can operate.

Recent research has indicated that whales can hear underwater sounds produced by other whales over distances of hundreds of miles, and it is not unreasonable to assume that many freshwater fish can detect vibrations at distances of several miles.

Sounds, or vibrations, travel much faster and more efficiently through water (which is incompressible) than they do through air, and it seems likely that the capabilities of fish to detect them far exceed what most anglers suppose.

The question 'Can fish hear?' is often asked. The answer is that they cannot detect most of the sounds generated above the surface. You can talk to someone on the bank, even shout, and the fish won't know. Even the sound of a shotgun is not detected. They can, however, detect certain above-surface noises or shocks. Strangely, the slam of a car door can scare fish at distances of 100 yards or more.

Sounds generated under water are detectable at immense distances. The crunching of gravel caused by a wading angler, banging on the gunwale of a boat, the vibrations of an outboard motor, are all readily detectable by fish, probably for miles. So are the vibrations caused by other fish swimming, and a variety of other sounds or vibrations. From these a fish gains as clear a picture of what goes on in its underwater world as a man gains of his surroundings by the use of his ears.

3. *Touch*

Not much is known about the sense of touch in fish, but it seems certain that species equipped with barbules, like carp, tench, barbel, gudgeon, roach and catfish, must use these appendages to locate their food – especially since these fishes are bottom-feeders and include in their diets a high proportion of small animals that live on or in the bottom layers.

It seems probable that the barbules can sense the movements below the surface of the bottom mud, or silt, of such creatures as burrowing nymphs, bloodworms (chironomid larvae) and aquatic worms, enabling the fish to suck in a mouthful of mud containing the animal or animals that were detected in this way. The fish then separates these creatures from the mud, most of which is ejected.

Although the barbules are sensitive, the mouths of fishes generally are not. Predatory species like pike, zander, perch, ruffe, bullhead and trout will swallow hard or prickly creatures such as snails, mussels, caddises in their cases and sticklebacks which, if their captors' mouths were sensitive, would be too painful to tackle. Even soft-mouthed fishes like chub, carp, tench, roach, bream, barbel and dace will eat hard foods. The way in which a chub can smash a hard-shelled, full-sized crayfish, plentifully equipped with sharp points, is quite astonishing.

These facts should serve to reassure the angler about the effectiveness of certain natural baits. They also help to explain why a fish can swim off seemingly unconcerned with a hook in its mouth.

4. *Smell*

'Have fish a sense of smell?' is another question frequently posed. For us, smelling is made possible by the presence of tiny particles in the air. Similar small particles can diffuse in water and there is no doubt that fish can detect them, though different species probably

For Dave Steuart to have taken this fine Stour roach means that the fish was deceived; so that its vision, its hearing, its sense of touch, and its ability to smell – protective mechanisms all – were circumvented by the skilful angler

vary very greatly in their ability to do so. An eel can detect a dead fish lying on the bottom of a lake, at a distance of at least 400 yards. Salmon are capable of detecting the scent of a human hand, when the degree of dilution is astronomically great.

It is likely that all freshwater fishes have this ability to detect substances in the water; but it does not follow that synthetic smells add attraction to the angler's bait. The natural smell of the bait is sufficient, though in certain circumstances, as for example when the water is thick and muddy, it may be wise to choose a bait whose natural smell is strong.

It is likely that pike can detect the smell of a dead herring or mackerel at a much greater distance than they can that of a dead roach or dace. In floodwater, gorgonzola or Danish blue cheese seems to attract chub better than milder cheese.

When the proprietary groundbait 'Pomenteg' was being developed, care was taken to include ingredients which were not only palatable to fish but spread their scent or flavour over a wide area. The object was to attract fish to the groundbaited place from great distances. Experience has shown that this aim was achieved.

Intelligence

On the question of intelligence in fish, anglers hold a wide range of views.

Recent research has produced some interesting information. It seems that fish are much better at distinguishing colours than shapes. When feeding selectively on particular organisms, which fish frequently do, they can distinguish small differences in size and colour but fail to detect quite large differences in shape and in the positioning of recognition points.

They can, however, learn from experience. Experiments with carp in Holland showed that carp which had been caught on rod and line, and returned to the same water, became about four times less likely to be caught on the same bait from the same water. When, however, the fish were transferred after capture to a different water, they were only twice less likely to be recaught on the same bait, showing that they associated the uncomfortable experience of being caught not only with the bait but also with the surroundings in which they took it. It seems likely that similar associations are made by other species of fish, though probably to different degrees.

Chub learn well and long remember baits on which they have been caught, whereas tench seem much slower to learn and there are many instances of the same tench being caught twice or even three times from the same swim in the same day on the same bait.

To generalize – the angler who wishes to catch fish consistently will do well to find out which baits have caught most fish from the waters he visits, and then to use different baits directly he notices a falling off in his catches and those of other anglers, since the more successful a bait is when first tried, the sooner the fish will learn to avoid it and the greater will be the number of fish that have learned this. It is not only the fish that flees in terror on seeing a bait on which it has been caught previously, that the angler will fail to catch, for the fear will be communicated to other fish that might otherwise have been willing to bite.

3 Baits and Tackle

Hookbaits

It cannot truthfully be said that there has been a great expansion in our knowledge about baits in the last thirty years or so. The use of maggot chrysalids has greatly expanded but there is nothing new about this, since they have been known as a useful bait for centuries.

Some advances have been made in baits intended for use on soft bottoms or bottoms covered with filamentous algae (silkweed, blanket weed, flannel weed, etc.). These include combined paste and crust, where a piece of crust is put on the bend of the hook, crumb side towards the shank, and paste built up around the shank, and touching the crumb side of the crust, in such proportion that the combination just, and only just, sinks, coming to rest on the surface of soft mud or bottom weed without sinking into it. This combined bait also has the advantage that the line is underneath and therefore less likely to touch the lips of a taking fish.

This principle can be retained whether plain breadpaste or a mixture of breadpaste with other material is used. It allows the use of softer paste without risk of the bait being thrown off the hook in casting, the crust part quickly becoming soft in the water. Also useful over soft or weedy bottoms is a flat slice of parboiled potato, which sinks with a swinging motion.

Recent developments in baits for barbel, chub and carp include the use of meat or additives; lightly boiled sausage; mixtures of sausage meat; chunks or cubes of tinned luncheon meat; proprietary pet foods; crab paste; crab body meat; finely minced fish and the like, with a breadpaste base. In carp fishing, especially, these meaty pastes have been useful in allowing anglers to keep ahead of the education of the fish.

Baits in quantity. Tackle of the finest quality. Hard work and a great deal of preparation are needed to succeed in the match-fishing circuit. Note the great lengths this angler has gone to in order to achieve maximum efficiency (*Alfred Pond*)

Chub caught on Dutch cheese by G. Berth-Jones

A method of protecting the hookbait from ducks, coots and moor-hens when floating crust is used for carp, is to dye the crust with green vegetable dye of the kind sold for colouring cake-icing and other foodstuffs. The birds appear indifferent to green crust (unless by chance they swim very near to it) whereas they will spot an undyed crust at a distance of 50 yards or more.

Groundbait

Although there have been some advances in hookbait, few anglers pay attention to the design of groundbait mixtures, being content with any rubbishy material provided it is cheap. Popular groundbaits consist of waste from biscuit factories, bakeries and dog-food makers ground to a fine powder. At best such groundbaits are inferior. All too often – because (owing to their nature) they fail to go where the angler thinks they have gone – they may actually attract fish *away* from the hookbait!

Incorrect choice and use of groundbait will result in smaller catches of fish. Because they do not understand groundbaiting, many anglers pay to make their catches poorer!

The primary purpose of groundbait is to induce the fish to eat what the angler can conveniently use for bait. Attraction of fish to a particular place is only a secondary reason for using groundbait.

A good groundbait should be capable of being made up in a variety of ways to suit different conditions, by the addition of more or less water to it in its dry state, and by the application of more or less hand pressure when squeezing it into balls. The angler should be able to make it into very tight, solid balls which will sink quickly to the bottom in fast deep water – there to diffuse slowly. If a ball of groundbait breaks up into several smaller pieces that are carried off by the current, fish will be attracted *away* from the angler's swim.

It should also be possible to make up groundbait very lightly, with just sufficient adhesion to allow it to be thrown the requisite distance, but so that it will break up when it hits the surface. In still water, small particles should spread quickly over a very wide area.

Such a groundbait cannot be made simply from cheap waste products. It needs ingredients having different sinking rates, different rates of absorbing water and different degrees of swelling when wetted. It took several years of experiment to arrive at the composition of one particular proprietary groundbait, 'Pomenteg', which has the additional advantage of being dehydrated, so that the weight

These are not secret essences but merely typical pre-baiting materials – in readiness for an attack by R.W., F.J.T. and F.B. on a Tring Reservoir's big bream

and bulk the angler has to carry is reduced considerably. Unfortunately the advantages of carefully contrived groundbaits such as this are not widely appreciated, and the majority of anglers continue to buy rubbish, much of it bulked out with sand.

Given a basic high-quality, multi-ingredient groundbait, various additives can often be used to increase its attractiveness and relate it to the hookbait. If cheese or cheesepaste is being used as a hook-bait for chub, a little dried powdered cheese, the kind caterers use for making cheese-straws and cheese biscuits, can be added to the groundbait.

For relating to breadcrust used as hookbait, cornflakes can be

The first of a number of 7 lb bream taken by F.J.T. and brother Ken after a three-day stint involving day- and night-fishing sessions. Some eighty stale loaves were used as groundbait

mixed with the groundbait. In tench fishing, oxblood, with an anti-coagulant added, can go into the groundbait, while the hookbait can be a sample of the groundbait stirred up with plenty of oxblood to which no anti-coagulant has been added; this is spread on a flat baking tray and allowed to set, after which it is cut into cubes.

There are plenty of other examples of adding suitable hookbait samples to groundbait, with great advantage; but it must always be understood that unless the groundbait goes where it is wanted, and unless the bulk of it stays there, it is better not to use groundbait at all. To help the angler to place the groundbait where he wants it, there are a number of cunning devices available.

Groundbaiting devices

Figure 1 illustrates a twin-celled plastic pike float. The upper cell is air-filled to provide buoyancy. The lower cell is perforated, to allow a supply of maggots to escape gradually and attract small fish round the livebait – an added attraction for the pike.

Figure 2 illustrates a boat with a polythene bait-delivery tube rigged overside. The tube is designed to deliver groundbait close to the bottom. This gives an angler the opportunity of swimming a baited hook just off the bottom in the middle of the groundbait trail. The bait-delivery tube can be adapted for bank fishing, and the tube combined with a hopper feed.

Figures 3 and 4 depict a bait-dropper – an adaptable device which can be used for 'lift-fishing', 'laying-on', 'float-ledgering', or 'swimming the stream'. It has two functions:

1. It deposits a load of maggots on to a selected part of the river or lake bed.
2. It carries the groundbait straight to the bottom, without attracting small and undesirable fish on the way down.

Most droppers have a cork fitted on one side to accommodate the angler's hook. This enables the angler to attach the bait-dropper to the end of his tackle without having to 'break down'.

Figure 3 depicts the loaded bait-dropper before it hits bottom. The striker releases the contents of the dropper as soon as it touches the river bed (*figure 4*). A bait-dropper must be swung out smoothly and easily with the rod, otherwise there is a danger of the groundbait tipping out. Because of this, dropper-techniques are associated with close-to-the-bank fishing.

Figures 5 and 6 show the swimfeeder, a device capable of depositing (at long range, if necessary) a quantity of maggots straight on to the lake or river bed. The maggots, contained within a sandwich of soft mash, are prevented from escaping until the water has dispersed the mash and freed them.

Figure 5 shows one of the best methods of attachment.

Figure 6 shows the action of the stream emptying the feeder, and illustrates the effect of hookbaits mixed with groundbaits. Seal one

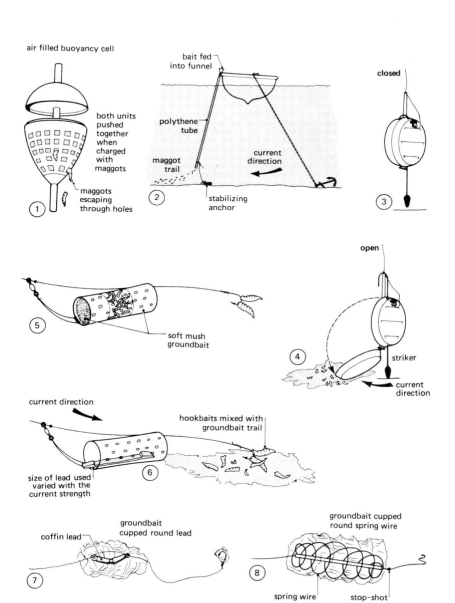

air filled buoyancy cell

both units pushed together when charged with maggots

maggots escaping through holes

(1)

bait fed into funnel

polythene tube

maggot trail

current direction

stabilizing anchor

(2)

closed

(3)

open

striker

current direction

(4)

soft mush groundbait

(5)

current direction

hookbaits mixed with groundbait trail

size of lead used varied with the current strength

(6)

coffin lead

groundbait cupped round lead

(7)

groundbait cupped round spring wire

spring wire

stop-shot

(8)

end of the feeder with mash. Fill the middle with maggots, and seal the other end with more mash.

Of all snares, a crust-baited hook used in conjunction with similar pieces of groundbait crust is the deadliest for large roach.

The swimfeeder provides a means of getting the crust groundbait straight down to the bed of a river. Without wetting or pressing, the springy nature of the crust ensures a grip on the inside wall of the feeder.

Figure 7 shows one of the oldest and simplest methods of ground-baiting. A mash of bread/bran (or similar groundbait), with or without a sprinkling of maggots, is 'cupped' round the ledger lead. Although this method is simple in operation, the angler must take great care when mixing his mash. An over-sloppy mixture tends to fly off during the cast, or when the lead hits the water; an over-stiff mixture may fail to break up at all.

Figure 8 shows a natural development of the 'cupping' method of groundbaiting: the springwire. This consists of a fine copper or brass tube soldered to a wire coil. This method is suitable for use by ledger anglers who fish at long range, because groundbait of any reasonable consistency readily adheres to a springwire even during the most violent casting. The springwire can be used effectively in conjunction with float tackle provided the angler is fishing in deep water. The greater the depth, the less the disturbance caused by splash when the bait-loaded wire is cast.

Figure 9 depicts, a comparatively new groundbaiting device: a transparent bag of soluble plastic (polyvinyl acetate, made by ICI).

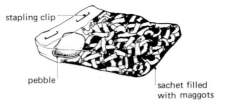

stapling clip

pebble

sachet filled
with maggots

Figure 9   Sachet groundbaiting

The sachet is filled with maggots, and a pebble included to over-come buoyancy of trapped air. The end of the bag is then staple-clipped. When thrown into a swim the bag, with enclosed maggots, sinks to the bottom. Within minutes it dissolves – leaving a concentration of maggots on the bed of the swim. The value of getting groundbait straight to the bottom, before small fish help themselves to it, is obvious.

In still water, the exact position of the groundbait can be marked by including a small quantity of sodium bicarbonate and citric acid in the sachet. As soon as water reaches the mixture, gas bubbles are generated. These bubbles, rising to the surface, provide the angler with a target at which he can aim his baited hook.

Figure 10 shows the Polycone, one of the most advanced of all swim-feeder designs. The cone's sharp nose causes less disturbance than the conventional, blunt-nosed, cylinder-shaped maggot-feeder. When stationary on the bottom, the body creates less drag, and during a strike reduces strain on rod and line.

The feeder can be used either for ledgering or float-ledgering. In both cases the mainline can be passed through an eye of a swivel that has been jammed in the apex of the cone. A stop-shot or a second swivel prevents the feeder from running down to the hook.

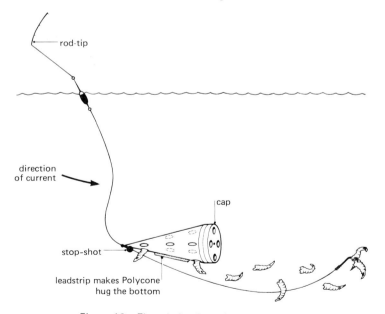

rod-tip

direction of current

cap

stop-shot

leadstrip makes Polycone hug the bottom

Figure 10   Float-ledgering with a Polycone

The feeder is loaded with maggots by means of a removable cap that fits over the blunt end. When in position on the river bed the maggots crawl out of the holes and are drifted by the current towards the hookbait. An alternative way of fitting a polycone is to fit a link of nylon (say 12 inches) between the swivel in the apex of the cone and a second swivel. The mainline to the hook is then passed through the end eye of the second swivel before a stop-shot or its equivalent is fitted.

The modern angler can equip himself with tackle far superior to anything formerly available. He does not always do so, failing to realize that it always pays to buy the best equipment available. This is not only cheapest in the long run; it is more effective and satisfying to use, and it invariably comes from a manufacturer who sets a high value on his reputation and the goodwill of his business. Complain about a defect in a cheap item of tackle and you will receive an indifferent answer, if you receive one at all. Advise a reputable firm of a defect in a quality item of tackle, and you will invariably receive fair and generous redress.

When considering the purchase of a rod, reel, line or other item of tackle, ask yourself how you would feel if, through saving a few pounds, you lost the fish of a lifetime. It would be too late then to change your mind. There is plenty of bad tackle in the shops. Let it stay there.

Rods

Nowadays there is a very wide range of coarse-fishing rods from which to choose, and it is difficult to imagine circumstances for which nothing suitable can be found. The last two decades have brought great changes in rod design, mainly through the introduction of fibreglass.

The first glass rods were not at all satisfactory, being made of straight-taper blanks of constant wall-thickness. This meant that, under stress, the cross-section tended to ovality and consequently the deflection of the rod increased, not in direct proportion to the load, but faster and faster as the load increased. These rods were compared unfavourably with split-cane rods, of which the opposite is true, and for many years after the introduction of hollow fibreglass, discriminating and experienced anglers found it unacceptable.

Fibreglass blanks built in Hardy's factory are stacked before the next operation of rod building

More recently, the characteristics of fibreglass as a rod material have been studied scientifically and the job of designing rods to be made from it has been tackled on a mathematical instead of a trial-and-error basis. Glass cloths with special weaves have been made available, with more longitudinal than circumferential fibres. Correct tapers have been calculated, and the use of these, together with varying wall-thicknesses, have eliminated the trouble of ovality.

The result is a range of rods that are much lighter than their split-cane predecessors. They can cast farther when necessary, while being well able to handle big fish. It is, however, necessary to remember that if one uses a lighter rod more force must be applied to set the hook regardless of the rod's power in casting. Failure to realize this (by anglers who have changed from split-cane to fibreglass) has resulted in many losses through hooks not being driven fully home.

It is often said that there is no craftsmanship in the manufacture of fibreglass rods, by comparison with that necessary for split-cane. In fact, the days when the sections of a split-cane rod were planed by hand, except by enthusiastic amateurs, have long gone, and there is no need to regret their passing. The machines used to cut the bamboo strips do the job far more accurately than is possible by hand (see *figure 11*).

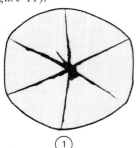
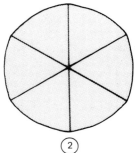

Figure 11   1. Showing an exaggerated drawing of a section built under the old method
2. Showing a drawing of an actual photograph of a section built under the improved method

Manual skills had been replaced by machinery long before the advent of fibreglass, but experience and judgement still remained essential for split-cane, and they are just as necessary for fibreglass – as a visit to a modern rod-maker will quickly demonstrate. A bad operator will make bad rods out of fibreglass as readily as he would have out of split-cane.

Many of the operations involved in making glass rods require every bit as much craftsmanship as was involved in producing rods of other materials. This is why the advent of glass has not substantially reduced prices, certainly in the case of the better-quality rods.

Nor has glass reduced the liability of a rod to break if it is misused. In the early days, we were told that glass rods were indestructible; you could beat down nettles with them or run them into brick walls without risk of breakage – it was said. That was to some extent true of solid fibreglass, from which heavy, floppy and altogether horrible rods can be made. It was never true of hollow glass, and nowadays a competent rod designer refuses to design rods that are proof against gross abuse, for to do so would result in weapons that would be totally unacceptable to an experienced and skilful modern angler. If you tread on a modern glass rod, or slam it in a car door, or use great violence to cast weights outside its designed range, you have every chance of smashing it.

Parallel with the development of better rod materials has been improvement in fittings; harder and stronger rings; better reel fittings; and above all, the development of spigot ferrules (see *figure 12*). If properly made and fitted, such ferrules are entirely trouble-free. They never stick or come loose on the rod material as metal ferrules so often do. All they need is the tiniest touch of paraffin or beeswax once a year, and even without it they function pretty well.

Figure 12

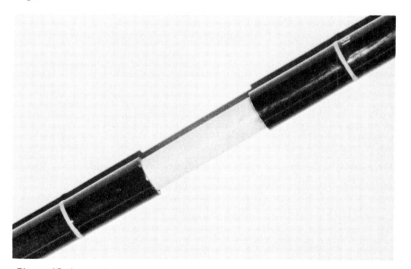

Figure 12 shows the type of ferrule used on the best split-cane rods, i.e. a splint-end suction ferrule. The splints cannot be seen as they are concealed beneath the whippings. Each splint (there are six) lies along the appropriate 'flat' of cane. Splints are flexible and help to reduce the strain that would otherwise be concentrated at the point where the cane enters the ferrule (female joint) or counter (male joint)
The lower picture shows the most modern method of joining fibreglass rod-sections, i.e. with a carbon-fibre reinforced spigot joint

They flex with the rod, they add only the tiniest amount of extra weight, and if after many seasons of hard use a little wear and looseness develops, it is simple to rectify.

The one area in which no progress has been made is fortunately one where none is needed, for it is unlikely that a better material for rod handles than cork will ever be found. It is light, firm, durable and capable of being shaped at will, and above all it gives a good grip, hot or cold, wet or dry. Its resilience permits the use of simple sliding reel fittings which, if provided with correct internal angles, hold a reel securely without complication.

Choice of rod

While there remains room for high-quality split-cane rods in trout fly-fishing, the angler buying a new coarse-fishing rod can confine his attentions to fibreglass, or carbon-fibre, though if he already possesses a good split-cane rod that has remained straight after many seasons of use, he may be wise to retain it, especially if he intends to use it in a branch of coarse fishing where it will spend most of its time in a rest.

Coarse fish may be divided conveniently into four categories:

1. Big carp and barbel
2. Bream, chub, tench, smaller carp, big perch
3. Roach, dace and rudd
4. Pike.

For the first category, where the style of fishing will usually be ledgering, a 10 ft two-piece rod having a test-curve of $1\frac{1}{2}$ lb is the best choice. Such a rod will take lines of from 6 lb to 12 lb BS (dry breaking strain) and cast leads of up to about $1\frac{1}{2}$ oz. It can thus be used for salmon and pike spinning, though it is not powerful enough for live-baiting with large baits, or deadbaiting with herrings or mackerel.

In recent years, it has been suggested that rods of 11 ft or 12 ft may have some advantage in carp fishing. In practice, such rods are generally held higher up the grip, so their effective length is not much greater; and if it is, there will be extra leverage against the angler's hand, which will the more quickly start to ache when a big fish is in play. A longer rod also reduces the pressure the angler can apply when that is necessary to keep a fish away from weed or snags.

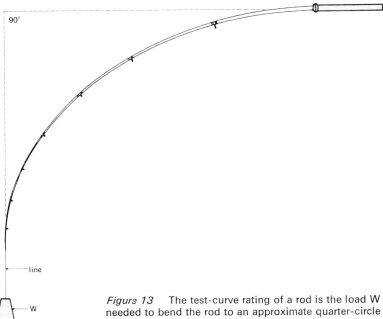

90°

line

W

Figure 13   The test-curve rating of a rod is the load W
needed to bend the rod to an approximate quarter-circle

A blank is tested for correct deflection

Consequently there is no reason for choosing a carp rod that is longer than 10 ft, except where fishing is to be done at extreme casting range.

It is important to choose one having correct tapers as well as a suitable test-curve, otherwise soft baits will not stay on the hook in casting.

For the second category, two kinds of rod are needed, for ledgering and float fishing. For ledgering, a 10 ft two-piece rod with a test-curve of about 1 lb will usually do all that is required; a somewhat steeper taper than that of the $1\frac{1}{2}$ lb test-curve carp rod is advantageous. This will throw up to 1 oz, but for ledgering at extreme range, as is sometimes necessary in lake fishing for bream and big perch, the carp rod can be used instead. The 1 lb test-curve rod will take lines from about $3\frac{1}{2}$ lb to 8 lb BS.

For float fishing and for some aspects of lighter ledgering, there is a choice of lengths of three-piece rods, with test-curves of about $\frac{3}{4}$ lb, though for long-trotting in fast water, where chub and barbel are found, a somewhat more powerful rod is needed with a 1 lb test-curve. For this, a rod of 11 ft to 12 ft is suitable. Ordinarily, a $\frac{3}{4}$ lb test-curve suffices and for easy, fatigue-free fishing a 12 footer is excellent. Only in special circumstances is there any advantage in a longer rod of 13 ft or even 14 ft. These longer rods are more tiring to use, but they are sometimes helpful in fishing over marginal weed-beds or rush-growths.

For the third category, the same range of three-piece rods will do well. These rods will take a wide range of line-strengths, from about 2 lb to 7 lb BS, and cast up to $\frac{3}{4}$ oz, but they behave very well with lightly-loaded tackle also.

For pike fishing, the 10 ft, $1\frac{1}{2}$ lb test-curve carp rod takes care of spinning with artificial lures, plugs, spoons and other spinners, up to $1\frac{1}{2}$ oz in weight, though the weight to consider is the combined weight of lure and lead, if any.

For much heavier baits like live or dead fish, or outsize plugs, again a 10 ft two-piece rod is recommended, but with a test-curve of $3\frac{1}{2}$ lb to 4 lb. This may also be useful for dealing with large carp in very snaggy or weedy conditions, where strong lines and hooks are also necessary and extreme pressure must be applied to hooked fish. Suitable lines run from 12 lb to 25 lb BS, and weights of up to $4\frac{1}{2}$ oz can be cast using the full power of the rod. More important, by the use of a long, slow, sweeping, casting action, it is possible to pitch baits weighing up to half a pound to sufficient distances, when these are needed to catch pike, and a rod of this power will pull home the larger hooks, or multiples of hooks, that are usually associated with these bigger baits.

Such a rod is also desirable for pike fishing in Irish and some Scottish waters where pike not only grow huge, but also fight, weight for weight, about three times harder than the pike found in southern England. On a water such as Loch Lomond there is always the possibility of hooking a pike of 30 lb, 40 lb or even 50 lb that will fight far, far harder than a fish from the Broads or the Thames. Consequently it is folly to use a line of less than 20 lb BS, or a rod that prevents the strength of such a line from being used to full advantage.

Those then are the kinds of rod that the all-round coarse-fish angler will require to be basically well equipped, though he may also wish to add more specialized rods to his armoury. The match angler may require rods that will take screw-in visual bite-indicators like swing-tips, spring-tips, or quiver-tips.

In this picture R.W. is fishing a Lincolnshire lake. Notice that he is using leg and forearm to support the rod – so as to make use of the *full* length of the rod

One sort of rod that is seldom seen used in coarse fishing is the fly rod, yet fly-fishing tackle can be used to deadly effect in certain conditions for many coarse-fish species, including roach, dace, rudd, chub and perch. The last-named is specially vulnerable to large two- or three-hook lures of the kind used in sea-trout and in reservoir trout fishing, used with a fast-sinking line. A minority of experienced anglers who have realized the value of fly fishing for coarse fish would consider two fly rods, one to take a No. 5 or No. 6 floating line for the more delicate requirements, and the other taking a No. 8 or No. 9 line for long casting and lure-fishing on bigger waters – essential equipment if full use of angling opportunities is to be made.

Reels

Never has there been so wide a choice of reels for freshwater fishing as there is now. For fly-fishing there are simple single-action reels, reels with geared drives, and automatic, or clockwork, reels. For general coarse fishing there are centre-pins, open-faced fixed-spool reels, closed-faced fixed-spool reels, and semi-closed-faced reels. For pike and salmon spinning there is the choice of fixed-spool reels, multipliers of various kinds, and large centre-pins.

Recently, the automatic fly reel has been extensively advertised. The great drawback to this kind of reel is its weight, which exceeds 12 oz even in the lightest models.

To add so much weight to rods which themselves weigh only from 3 oz to 5 oz is to cause butt-heaviness which interferes with correct casting and involves a good deal of fatigue for the angler. In addition, the amount of line such reels will recover, though in general adequate for river and stream fishing, is insufficient for lakes and reservoirs, and should a manufacturer decide to design an automatic reel with a much larger recovery capacity, the additional weight involved would make its use intolerable. As rods become lighter, it becomes easier to throw away that advantage by the use of over-heavy reels. This applies to all branches of freshwater fishing including trout fishing, and it will soon be necessary for reel designers to pay much more attention to the need for lightness than they have done in the past.

There is much to be said for the type of multiplying fly reel that has a modest gear ratio of less than 2 to 1. It permits a useful reduction in diameter and therefore in weight, while retaining an adequate rate of line recovery, and a capacity to house sufficient flyline for most fly-fishing if backed by nylon monofil. Simple single-action fly reels are however, quite adequate for most purposes. In any fly reel, an exposed flange for the drum is advantageous.

The position of the reel on the rod handle is important. Many coarse-fishing rods have comparatively long cork grips which are provided to allow the angler to position his reel in a way that suits his stature. We often see reels so placed that a foot of cork handle is projecting behind the angler's elbow while he is holding the rod above the reel. This wastes much of the effective length of the rod.

For general coarse fishing the most useful reel is the open-face, conventional fixed-spool. Two types are used, one of medium size with a capacity of about 200 yards of 12 lb BS monofil and a gear ratio of about $3\frac{1}{2}$ or 4 to 1; and a smaller version for use with finer lines, down to about 2 lb BS, with a higher gear ratio of between 5 and 6 to 1. In choosing such reels, look for a smooth slipping-clutch mechanism; a clockwise direction of rotation for the pick-up as seen from the front of the spool, if you are right-handed; a rotating roller in the pick-up line guide; an even distribution of the line on the spool; and a design which enables the forefinger to reach and control the spool easily when the reel is on a rod.

Closed-faced and semi-closed-faced reels have the single advantage that the line is less likely to get where it shouldn't be, and this helps in windy conditions. These reels are, however, very bad for playing big fish, because the pull in the line must be reduced greatly before any line can be recovered, owing to the friction produced at the many angles through which the line must pass. In addition, finger-control of the spool is impossible.

Technically, no advantages are to be found in centre-pin reels. They are pleasant to use, once the necessary skills have been acquired, but nostalgia accounts for much of their popularity.

For pike and salmon spinning, the large centre-pin is still favoured by some anglers; but the superiority of the multiplier, with its 4 to 1 gear ratio and small-diameter spool, or perhaps with a slightly lower ratio in the case of the small sea multipliers so useful for fishing heavy natural baits for pike, is undeniable.

Large fixed-spool reels can also be used but generally speaking the bigger a fixed-spool reel, and the heavier the line used on it, the less satisfactory it becomes.

More often than not, the higher price asked for the best-quality reels is well justified and in the long run such reels are actually cheaper as well as being more efficient and pleasant to use, though it is only fair to say that, with any reel, trouble is more likely to stem from neglect, misuse or accidental damage than from inherent defects.

Lines

Monofilament

Monofilament line must be the best value for money throughout the vast range of modern fishing tackle. Unlike the older plaited silk and so-called gut-substitute lines, monofilament is consistent in strength and diameter throughout its spool length. Or *should* be. One occasionally hears of unexpected weaknesses and breakages – but there is always a reason for these inconsistencies. Age, exposure to strong light, abnormal friction or pressure all affect the strength of a monofilament line, and these factors should be considered while a line is in use.

The trouble is, of course, that most monofilament lines *are* so reliable. And because of this their age and the amount of usage they get are forgotten. They still *look* good, even after several years of hard fishing, and the angler assumes that they still *are* good. As a result he tends to fish through season after season with the same line, until it loses so much of its original length that is *has* to be replaced.

This is a very false economy. Hooks aside, the line is the most important item of tackle. Monofilament should be renewed at least once a year. There would be far fewer breakages (and disappointments over lost fish) if this were a regular practice. After all, monofilament is cheap enough.

In choosing nylon, pick a kind that strikes a sensible compromise between tractability and strength. Many ultra-strong monofils are not very shock-resistant and although stronger against a steady strain break very easily on a sudden jerk. The colour is of little importance.

Unlike lines of silk and flax, monofilament needs no drying; but any sign of white powdery substance on the spool is a warning of corrosion. This occurs after long storage; also, if the monofilament

The record catfish (43 lb 8 oz) caught by Richard Bray of Chesham while fishing Wilstone Reservoir in September 1970 (F. Guttfield)

is used in salt water and the spool is not thoroughly cleaned in fresh water afterwards. Fine lines are, of course, more susceptible to this kind of deterioration. Heavy monofilament will tolerate more corrosion than a line of, say, 3 or 4 lb BS. Corrosion or oxidization will reduce the diameter of a thick line by only a small percentage; it may well reduce a thinner one by 50 per cent or more.

Monofilament is ideal for fixed-spool reels and suitable for use with multiplying and centre-pin reels. It can be used for all methods of fishing except fly-fishing. In certain circumstances, however, braided line is preferable.

Braided lines

At long range, stretch in a monofilament line is such that most of the strike is absorbed. A braided line helps to overcome this disadvantage. (Some of the big spoon baits sold today are very attractive to fish, but often fail because their large trebles are hard to set.)

Braided lines are usually made of dacron or nylon. Both are good, but because braided dacron has less stretch than braided nylon it obviously has an advantage when it comes to setting hooks – *provided the rod in use is powerful enough.* Clearly, there is little point in using dacron and large hooks with a weak rod.

Braided line is not suitable on fixed-spool reels, but because it is buoyant and comparatively inelastic we recommend it for big-bait spinning and for long-range livebaiting and deadbait float-ledgering.

A point to remember is that American braided lines nearly always break *before* their supposed limit has been reached. In our experience, 20 lb BS lines have broken at 15–17 lb. Other lines have broken at proportionately more or less. This is because certain American fish records are judged in relation to the breaking strain of the line used. If a line breaks at above its specified breaking strain the record cannot be accepted. American tackle manufacturers are therefore at great pains to ensure that their lines break at *less* than the stated test. British manufacturers, on the other hand, are anxious that their lines should break *above* the stated test; if the lines are slightly thicker than normal, no one minds.

Trouble starts when an angler buys a spool of American braided line (say 20 lb BS) because it looks so much finer than British line of the same supposed strength. It is undoubtedly thinner than its British counterpart, but it breaks at 17 lb – whereas the British line breaks at 23 lb. American line marked at 25 lb BS is about as thick as British 20 lb line. But both break at 23 lb! These figures are hypothetical, but they serve to explain the situation.

The life of braided lines is longer than that of the average monofilament line, and they deteriorate less under tension. They are considerably dearer but, in the higher breaking strains, they are probably worth it. This is specially so if they are to be put on to reels that are used only a few times each season. They can be left for several years without fear of deterioration.

Note: Remember that braided lines need special knots. More attention than there is room for here is given to them in Falkus and Buller's *Freshwater Fishing* (Macdonald and Jane's, 1974), p. 416.

Hooks, leads and swivels

Hooks

Contrary to popular supposition, hooks are seldom driven fully home when the angler strikes. Penetration is only *started* then. It is completed while the fish is being played. Only very small hooks penetrate almost immediately.

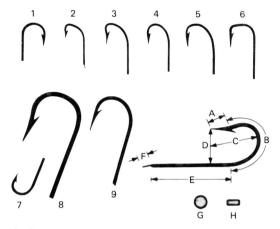

Figure 14   Hook patterns
A hook is generally recognized by the shape of its bend. The commonest types are shown here

1. The Round bend
2. The Crystal bend
3. The Limerick bend
4. The Kirby bend
5. The Sproat bend
6. The Sneck bend
7. The Kendal Round bend
8. The Round bend (deep throated)
9. The Model Perfect bend

The various parts of a hook are named:

A barb
B bend
C throat or bite
D gape
E shank
F eye or spade
G regular wire section
H forged wire section

The pull is never in line with the hook-shank, no matter what means are used for attaching the hook to the monofil. The initial pull acts along a line joining the hook-point to the eye (or spade), but changes as the hook penetrates, changing to a line joining the eye and the point on the bend to which penetration has reached. Clearly, the limit of depth to which the hook can penetrate is reached when it has gone in to the place on the bend that is most remote from the eye.

There is no advantage in having the hook-point other than parallel to the shank. In-curved and out-point hooks offer no advantages. The in-curved hook penetrates more easily but takes a shallower hold. The out-point requires more force to effect penetration, and the leverage tending to open out the hook is greater.

The barb should be nearer to the point than to the bend; not cut to a depth of more than about 10 per cent of the wire thickness, and not turned up too far. An angle between point and barb of 30 degrees is quite enough.

There is no advantage in up- or down-turned eyes; a straight ring eye suffices, but it must be properly closed. Alternatively, a spade-end may be used. A simple round-bend design, whose shank, measured from eye to outside of bend, is about two and a half times the gape, is as good as any and better than most.

Few hooks are as sharp as they might be when bought. Consequently, improvement in sharpness is always possible and it is advisable to touch up all hook-points with a small sharpening stone, the best kind being an Arkansas stone. Other than for bony-mouthed fishes, a hook cannot be too sharp. Not only should the points of new hooks be touched-up before they are used, they should be checked frequently while fishing is in progress.

Hooks should also be tested for correct tempering before being used. A good hook should be springy, returning to its original shape when pressure deflecting any part of it is released. If the bend is gripped, it should be possible to deflect the shank by about 30 degrees and on release, see it return to its former position. If it does not, the hook is over-tempered (too soft). If the hook breaks, it is under-tempered (too hard).

At this point it may be helpful to explain the heat treatment of straight carbon steels, of which hooks are made. The steel is first heated to a bright red colour, then it is quenched rapidly. This brings the steel to its maximum hardness, which is much too brittle for fish-hooks. Therefore, the hardness is reduced by re-heating to the correct temperature and allowing the metal to cool slowly. This second process of heating and cooling is known as tempering, and it is much more difficult to carry out correctly than the initial hardening, which is why too many hooks are too brittle or too soft.

Where the hook is covered with the bait, its colour and finish are not important; otherwise, there might be something to say in favour of metallic finishes which reflect the underwater environment. It is very doubtful, however, if the finish of the hook has any bearing on the angler's catch.

The size of hook depends on the bait in use, the need for strength to deal with large fish, and the strength of line to which the hook is attached. It is unwise to try to drive in a big hook with too fine a line, whereas a small hook carrying a small bait will behave unnaturally on a strong, thick line. For general coarse fishing, the range of sizes 2 to 16 suffices. Match anglers tend to use smaller hooks, sizes 18 and 20, and lose many good fish because of it.

Leads

The obvious function of a fishing lead is to sink and, if necessary, anchor the bait. Many leads, however, have auxiliary functions and are designed accordingly. *Figure 15* depicts a selection.

15.1 *The traditional plummet.* As its name implies, it is used to plumb the depth of a swim.

15.2 *The modern plummet.* Originally of French origin, this consists of two spring-loaded cups centrally hinged. Pressure on the two 'ears' opens these cups sufficiently to allow a baited hook to be dropped inside. When the pressure is released, the cups close over the baited hook. Before the traditional plummet can be used, the bait must usually be removed. The modern plummet avoids this delay.

15.3 *The coffin lead* (ledgering).

15.4 *The drilled-bullet lead* (ledgering).

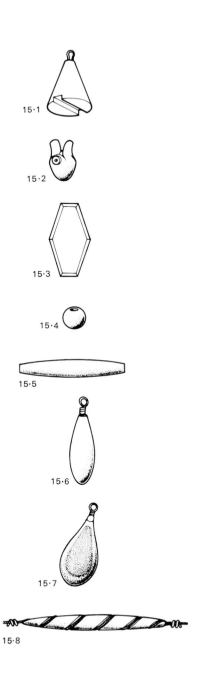

15·1

15·2

15·3

15·4

15·5

15·6

15·7

15·8

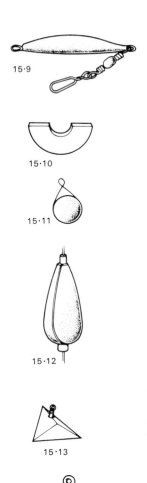

15·9

15·10

15·11

15·12

15·13

15·14

15·15

15.5 *The barleycorn or barrel lead* (ledgering).

15.6 *The Arlesey bomb* (ledgering). The Arlesey bomb, though not invented by R.W., was redesigned and popularized by him in the early 1950s. He produced this design of lead especially for long-distance casting to the big perch that were almost out of range in Arlesey Lake, Bedfordshire. For the first time in angling history a lead was designed after full consideration of the relevant aero-dynamic problems. (After gravity, air-resistance is the chief limiting factor to distance casting.)

The Arlesey bomb will not tumble in flight. As a result it is less likely to foul line and tackle during its passage through the air. The built-in swivel prevents kinks developing in the line. On the bed of a lake or a slow moving river, the Arlesey bomb stands nearly upright. This is a useful design feature, since it helps to keep the line clear of mud.

The Arlesey bomb is very useful when bait and lead are required to bounce and roll over the bed of a river. The swivel almost entirely eliminates the chance of the lead kinking or fouling the line.

15.7 *Arlesey bomb with flattened sides.* This is a useful lead to use in medium or fast rivers when an angler wishes to anchor his bait rather than have it move downstream. The more bulbous shape reduces casting range but improves anchoring efficiency.

15.8 *The Jardine lead* (spinning). This is a quick-change lead which can be put on a leader or removed without the tackle having to be broken down.

15.9 *The Wye lead* (spinning). This, too, can be removed easily if placed between two link-swivels (*figure 16*).

Figure 16

Figure 15 Some Arlesey bombs in $\frac{1}{4}$ oz, $\frac{1}{2}$ oz, 1 oz and $1\frac{1}{2}$ oz sizes will be wanted for general ledgering; some barleycorn leads for pike tackles, and some Wye leads for spinning. Sizes as for Arlesey bombs

15.10   *The half-moon lead* (spinning).   The half-moon is a useful lead for light spinning. It is the favourite lead of the fisherman who spins for trout, sea trout, or salmon in low-water summer conditions It is particularly useful for fishing in comparatively shallow streams, where a very light lead that also acts as an anti-kink is required.

15.11   *The Hillman lead* (spinning).   This, also a quick-change lead, is used with a swivel (*figure 17*).

leader   line

Figure 17   NB: Anti-kink lead is fixed to the *line end* of the swivel

15.12   *The Catherine lead.*   Another quick-change lead. For the angler who wishes to deadbait (with or without a float) and to use a lead, this is the best one for the job. The Catherine lead is slotted; so is the tapered hollow plastic peg that runs through its middle. This allows passage for the line through both slots into the bore of the plastic peg. Once the line is inside, the plastic peg is revolved ten degrees to close up the inner slot. Finally, the tapered peg is pushed tight into the lead – which is now free to be moved up and down the leader until located in the desired position by means of a stop-knot.

A pike picking up a deadbait is free to take line through a Catherine lead without moving the lead and without feeling its resistance. There are times when a fish may be sufficiently circumspect for such sensitivity in a rig to be important.

The pike angler who fishes with float tackle usually fits a Jardine lead, although a barrel lead is preferable since it is more secure. A barrel lead can be moved up and down the leader once a stop-shot is fitted.

15.13   *The Capta lead.* It is a lead of quite modern design. It has leech-like qualities because of its streamlined shape and will stay where it is on a river bed when heavier leads would be swept away. Aerodynamically, however, its shape makes it an inferior casting lead.

15.14   *The paternoster or pear lead.* This, like the Arlesey bomb, stands nearly upright on a river bed.

15.15 *The split-shot dispenser.*   A useful piece of equipment so long as an angler is able to purchase a refill of *any* size that gets used up.

Good-quality split shot is made of *soft* lead and nearly bisected by the cut that forms the split. Only if the lead is suitably soft can a shot be removed from the line and used again.* With large shot (see arrowed shot in *figure 18*) it helps if the leading edges are trimmed to form a 'V' entry to the split. This 'V' entry gives the fingernail greater purchase and facilitates the easy removal of shot from a leader without the need of a special tool.

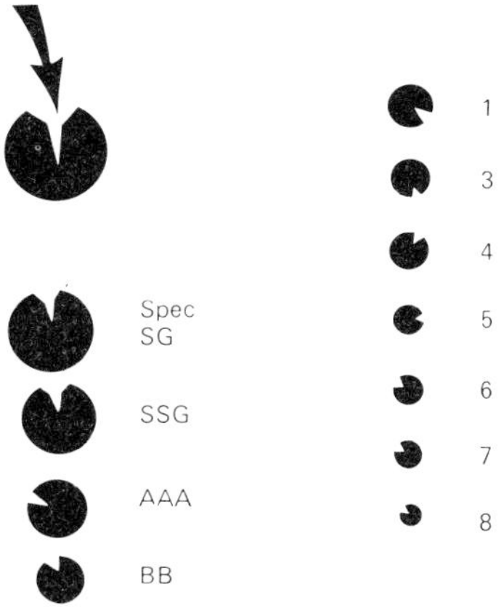

Name or Number	Pellets per ounce
Special SG	11
SSG	15
AAA	35
BB	70
1	100
3	140
4	170
5	220
6	270
7	340
8	450

Figure 18   Shot chart
A quantity of split shot will be required. If sizes SSG, AAA, BB, No. 3 and No. 6 are chosen, every contingency is covered, since one SSG weighs the same as two AAAs, four BBs, eight No. 3s or 16 No. 6s

Split shot of the same size should be uniform in weight. This uniformity is very important: it allows an angler to predetermine the number of shots that each of his floats will carry, thus eliminating the need for experiment at the bankside. All floats can be marked accordingly – thus guaranteeing that the nominated number of shots will cock the float nicely.

Swivels

A swivel's primary function is to minimize line-kink, but it can also be used as a link between separate parts of a rig. For instance, a wire leader is seldom joined direct to the main line. Instead, a swivel is

*Hard shot can be improved by cutting deeper.

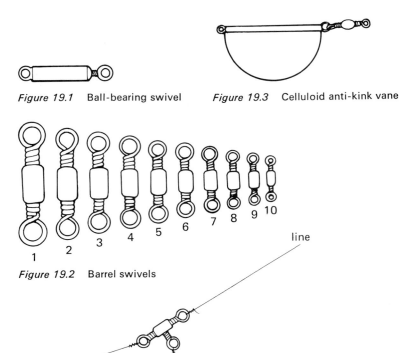

Figure 19.1   Ball-bearing swivel

Figure 19.3   Celluloid anti-kink vane

Figure 19.2   Barrel swivels

line

hookbait

lead

Figure 19.4   The three-way swivel correctly set up

Figure 19.5   Link swivel

Figure 19.6   Hardy's 'diamond-eye' swivel is an old favourite. It is made in two patterns: a link version and plain (as illustrated). The makers claim that the diamond-eye swivel is superior on two counts:

1. Friction is reduced to a minimum
2. Attachment to the swivel is central with the bearing

We think this pattern is superior to the more popular box and barrel swivels

interposed, and the line and the leader are fastened to opposite ends. Sometimes a link-swivel is preferred (*figure 19.5*) to facilitate a quick change of tackle.

The ball-bearing swivel (*figure 19.1*) is the most efficient, though it is not available in a series of graded sizes like the barrel swivel (*figure 19.2*), and it is comparatively expensive. But it is unhesitatingly recommended for spinning.

Fast-revolving baits often overload even a ball-bearing swivel, and then a swivelled anti-kink vane (*figure 19.3*) becomes essential.

Figure 19.4 illustrates a three-way swivel, popular for paternostering. Note that the mainline is tied to the link opposite the bait-link. Only the lead should be attached to the central side-link, otherwise the strain of playing a large fish will cause the swivel to warp and fracture.

The diamond-eye swivel, depicted in *figure 19.6* is an alternative pattern. Small, strong and efficient, it is made of rustless bright wire unlike the others, which usually have a natural or bronzed finish.

Nets

Landing Nets

Virtually all landing nets have disadvantages that stem from the compromise made between functional requirements and portability. The ideal net for most forms of angling would have a strong 5 ft handle, with a spike at one end and a rigid oval frame of ample dimensions at the other.

Fibreglass has now been exploited in making stronger, longer and lighter landing-net handles – which have the advantage of floating if they accidentally fall into the water. Incidentally, the same applies to nearly all hollow fibreglass rods; they float, even with a reel attached.

A 5 ft handle is easily carried. It can be used as a wading staff, and enables fish to be netted easily over marginal vegetation or from steep banks.

Unfortunately, permanently attaching a rigid net-ring of a diameter of 18 inches upwards to a 5 ft handle makes an assembly that is very difficult to transport to and from the waterside. A detachable or folding net-frame is desirable. A recent development consists of providing a strong plastic moulding with three holes. The shaft is pushed into the largest hole and two tubular fibreglass arms (carrying the net-mesh and joined by a stout plaited nylon thong) go into the other two holes. The result is an exceptionally light but strong assembly.

Folding, flip-up nets are favoured by many anglers, but their short handles and an element of unreliability in their folding and locking mechanisms are disadvantageous.

As regards size, a round, oval or triangular net of 20 to 24 inches in diameter suffices for most British freshwater species except large pike, salmon, carp, catfish and exceptionally large barbel and zander. For these larger species, a 30-inch net is desirable. Fashion rather than function has led to the production of nets as wide as 48 or even 60 inches, but this is affectation. The largest fish ever likely to be captured in British freshwaters will easily go into a 30-inch landing net.

Keepnets

A keepnet is a receptacle for keeping fish alive. An angler should choose a net that will house the size and number of fish he hopes to catch. All nets should have a fine mesh (gudgeon or even minnow mesh). This makes them suitable for housing small fish as well as big fish. All keepnets cause some pectoral and tailfin damage to fish. Fine mesh helps to reduce this damage.

The introduction of knotless-mesh keepnets that have a far less damaging effect upon fish is most satisfactory, since knotted nylon keepnets inflict appalling damage upon fish and are responsible for heavy (but unfortunately largely unseen) mortalities.

F.B., who has had considerable experience as a match angler, always carried two keepnets, one of which was held in reserve in case of a field day. The second net was also useful in the 'roving match' once popular in the south of England. It enabled the angler to rove without taking the bulk of his catch about with him.

If the angler can allow himself the luxury of fishing in one swim and hanging his keepnet in another he should do so even if it necessitates carrying the fish a dozen yards to the net. It is possible that disturbance caused by fish in a keepnet is communicated to other fish and deters them from feeding (at least it seems to deter the big ones!)

The reader who thinks this unlikely should remember that thousands of highly skilled match anglers fish every weekend – and

Round keepnets are bad for large fish, which get bent round in the shape of the net — like this catch of barbel

The rectangular net allows fish to keep their noses to the stream and lie in a natural position

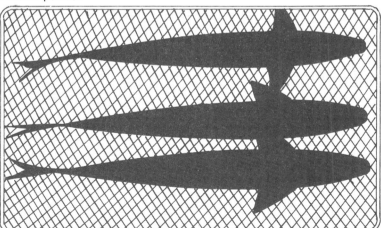

rarely catch a 2 lb roach between them during the whole season. Yet the waters they fish yield a number of 2 lb roach when all is quiet. Although of course there are other reasons why big roach are not caught on match days, it is almost certain that the main reason is water disturbance.

A keepnet is described as having depth, width and length. It should be long enough to accommodate the longest fish the angler is likely to catch. Such fish should be able to lie in the net in the normal horizontal position. Good nets are rectangular so that a number of fish of the same length can lie side by side. This shape of net allows the fish to face the stream in a natural position.

Round keepnets are bad because large fish are bent round in the shape of the net. A keepnet should have a long neck that can be used as a delivery funnel for the fish. This will eliminate the need to raise the net out of the water each time a freshly caught fish is put in.

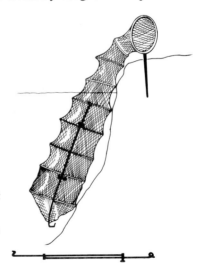

Figure 20   Keepnets should be large and made of knotless netting. They will need screw-in bank sticks. The keepnet stretcher – shown both separately and fitted to the keepnet – is designed to hold keepnets rigid in shallow swims. It also prevents a keepnet from collapsing on unseen underwater snags

Fitting instructions: Fit the ringed end of the stretcher on the fourth or fifth frame-wire (counting from the bottom) and place the hooked end on the wire handle at the bottom of the net (that part of the handle that is threaded through the net). After loosening the wing-nut, the stretcher is expanded to the appropriate tension and the wing-nut is re-tightened

The part of the net that houses the fish (the large rectangular or square section) should be fitted with a stretcher. There will then be no chance of the net failing to open out if it gets caught on an underwater obstruction.

A keepnet should be fitted with a rope and a bankstick-fitting so that it can be dangled to its plimsoll line even from a very high bank position (see *figure 20*).

4 Ledgering

When casting distance, water depth, speed of current, the nature of the river bottom, or any one of a dozen other factors makes float fishing impracticable, it becomes necessary to use the ledger. Before deciding whether to change from float to ledger tackle, however, it is worth while considering this simple question: Is *either* necessary? In other words, is there any need to load the tackle with leads, shots, quills or balsa strips? Cannot the bait be presented more naturally on a completely floatless and leadless tackle? Very often it can; and if this tackle is regarded as the *basic* rig to be used whenever possible, then situations demanding floats, leads, and other line attachments soon become apparent.

For any of the reasons already mentioned, it may be necessary to remove the float and add extra lead weight to the line. This may be needed for holding bottom in a fast current; casting a long way; getting a bait down in water much deeper than the rod, or to ensure that the bait is fishing on the bottom where the contours are uneven. In many of these situations float fishing can sometimes be un-manageable.

When a bait has to be fished hard on the bottom and held in a tight area, the ledger will take care of it. When the bait has to be rolled or bumped, along or across the bottom, through a shoal of bottom-feeding fish, the *correctly loaded* ledger will allow it to do so in a natural manner. Because extra lead has to be concentrated on the line, however, provision has to be made for the line to run freely through it. Theoretically at least, a fish pulling on the line should not move the lead because it is not fixed like a split shot but slides freely down to a stop-shot.

Old fashioned ledger leads little-used today have holes drilled right through them. Coffin leads, flat, heavy, and insensitive, settle hard and anchor the bait firmly. Round, bored bullets are little better.

They can be kept on the move but the line still passes right through them and makes for poor bite registration. Streamlined, swivelled leads of the Arlesey bomb-type cast well, do not tangle and, as the line only passes through the swivel eye, there is less friction and therefore less resistance to a biting fish.

Whatever lead is used, however, there is no guarantee that the line will slip through it all the time. There are situations where the current and direction of cast have a great deal of influence on the so-called sliding-ledger (see *figure 21*).

It becomes necessary then to devise a rig which is adjustable to fine limits and the nylon link-ledger is ideal. It comprises a few inches of thick nylon which is folded over the reel line and loaded with swan shots (see p. 59) AAs or BBs depending on the current. It should just and only just hold bottom in the current. Adjustment is made by adding or removing shots to or from the nylon link. As

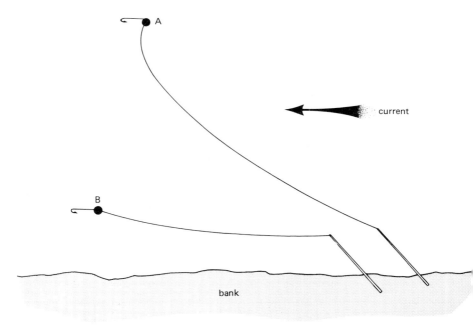

Figure 21   Diagram showing how the indication of a bite on ledger tackle depends on where the ledger is fished. A fish turning downstream with a bait (A) will cause a 'slack-line' bite. A fish doing the same thing at (B) will produce a positive pull

with laying-on, the length of 'trail' between hook and lead depends on the bait being fished and the bites expected.

A 4 or 5 ft trail will, in a fast current, allow the bait to rise and fall attractively. In mild weather and relatively high water temperatures, fish like chub and barbel may be swimming at any depth. The long trail covers water from bottom to a foot or so above. When cold conditions cause it to swim deeper and more slowly, the bait should be anchored or allowed to work close to the bottom on a short link. A bait wavering in the current may easily be unseen by a bottom-hugging fish (see *figure 22*).

Bite registration can be seen on the rod-tip or felt on the line; it is a matter of personal choice. There are no rules on the subject. Wherever possible, however, it is better to hold the rod and *feel* the line tighten (or slacken, as is often the case) when a bite comes (see p. 79). Where bites are few and far between it is less tiring to put the rod in a rest and watch the tip.

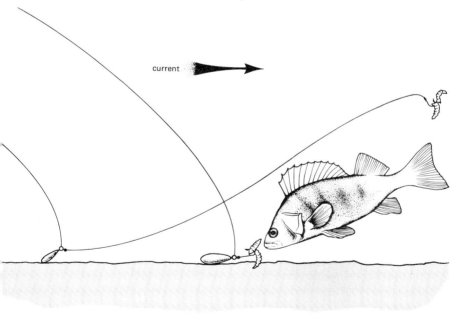

current

Figure 22 This diagram shows how a long-link ledger tackle may be relatively ineffective when, owing to low water temperature, the fish are hugging the bottom. In these circumstances it is best to use a short-link ledger

Special aids like swing-tips, quiver-tips and other forms of mechanical bite-indication are useful in certain circumstances, but the angler who relies upon them entirely and does not bother to learn the delicate skill of touch-ledgering will never be able to exploit ledgering to the full.

The Link-ledger

Fishing can be regarded as an art, a sport or a science, depending on one's philosophy. But it becomes more of a science when we try to find the reasons *why* we fish with a particular rig or method at a particular time.

A novice can be given any tackle rig and taught *how*, *where* and *when* to use it. But he will be helped a lot more if he can be told *why* he is using it.

Why, for instance, do certain methods work better on one water than another? Why does a certain bait prove more effective at certain times of the year? Why is a certain rig deadly for some fish and not others? Hundreds of books are devoted to the different methods of catching fish, but few offer information as to *why* they are used.

It is, of course, essential to learn *how* to float-fish, ledger, long-trot, lift-fish, lay-on, spin, deadbait, livebait, paternoster, stret-peg and so forth, but the beginner also needs to know which method he should choose at any particular time and, if he is intelligent, he will want a *reason* for choosing it.

For instance, it often pays to use a small bait on a short-link ledger for winter chub. Why?

It is generally true that, in very cold weather, fish, although willing to feed, do not require as much food as they do when the water is warmer. Because a fish is less active in cold water it is not likely to burn up as much energy and, for that reason, it will not need as much food, so that a smaller bait than usual presented close to the bottom is likely to be more successful than a large bait fished higher off the bottom.

A short-link ledger is used because it anchors the bait close to the bottom and holds it in one place. Chub, not being very active in these conditions, tend to hug the bottom and are unlikely to chase after food which wavers about in the current on a long link. It is likely that a bait attached to a long-link tackle would be overlooked.

The link-ledger tackle is used because it is simple to make and

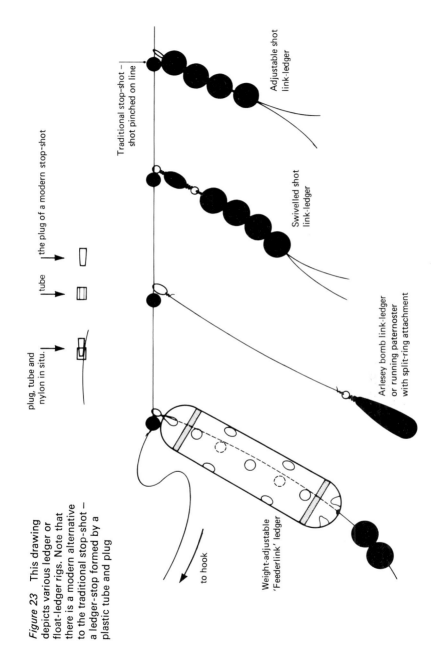

Figure 23 This drawing depicts various ledger or float-ledger rigs. Note that there is a modern alternative to the traditional stop-shot — a ledger-stop formed by a plastic tube and plug

plug, tube and nylon in situ.

the plug of a modern stop-shot

tube

Traditional stop-shot — shot pinched on line

Adjustable shot link-ledger

Swivelled shot link-ledger

Arlesey bomb link-ledger or running paternoster with split-ring attachment

Weight-adjustable 'Feederlink' ledger

to hook

is probably the most efficient ledger in use today. The separate nylon link is made up of a few inches of nylon considerably thicker than the reel line and loaded with several swan shots.

But *why* is the nylon link made of heavier nylon? *Why* does the loading have to be a number of split shots instead of one big lead? And *why* are the link ends not tied in knots so that the shots are more securely fixed?

(It is significant that such a simple piece of tackle can pose so many questions.)

The nylon link is thicker because it makes a firmer loop for the reel line to slip through. The line should slip through the link because fish are able to sense the resistance of a heavy lead, and although it isn't always possible to make provision for free passage of line through the link, it is always advisable to try to reduce resistance to a minimum. Fish, especially chub, can eject a bait very quickly, and what seems to be a good bite on ledger tackle is often caused by the fish *spitting out* the bait!

Lead is needed to anchor the bait, but because current variation and other factors often prevent the sliding link from functioning perfectly every time, the amount of lead must be adjusted to suit the current. It should settle lightly and remain in position just (but only just) holding against the pull of the current, and its grip on the bottom should be delicate enough for a biting fish to move without feeling resistance.

With certain adjustments to the weight the ledger can be fished upstream, across, or downstream. The simplest way to effect these adjustments is to add or remove the required number of swan shots. They'll slide quite easily off the open-ended link, but they wouldn't if the ends were knotted. Likewise, when a snag is encountered it is often possible to free the rest of the tackle by pulling hard and sliding the shots off the link. That's better than pulling for a break, and is often an added safety factor.

F.J.T. remembers playing a salmon in a Scottish river while his shot-link ledger was jammed between two big rocks. The line ran freely back and forth through the link while he gave and recovered line. Eventually the shots slid off the link leaving him to play the fish on a free and weightless line. A sliding bullet or any kind of fixed lead would probably have stayed jammed, and although he might have played his fish to a standstill, he could never have reached it with gaff or landing net. It would have been a complete stand-off with him on the bank and a beaten fish several yards out in the river. (The incident is remembered every time he makes up a link-ledger!)

It is unlikely that this could happen on an English river with a winter club attached, but it serves to illustrate how versatile the link-ledger can be, and answers yet another of the never-ending angling '*whys*'.

Bite-indicators

There are three basic types of bite-indicator: *visual, auditory* and *tactile*. An angler can *see* a bite, *hear* a bite and *feel* a bite.

1. *Visual*: The doughbobbin. (The float is the obvious example of a visual bite-indicator – but we have dealt with that separately.)
2. *Auditory*: The electric bite-alarm.
3. *Tactile*: Touch-ledgering.

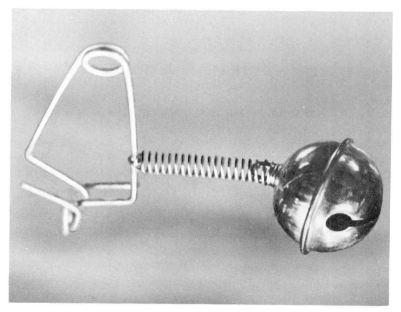

Auditory bite-indication in the shape of the peg-bell has long been the pier and beach angler's delight.

The doughbobbin

As the name implies, the doughbobbin can be made from a dollop of breadpaste or dough or, of course, more durable materials (*figure 24*).

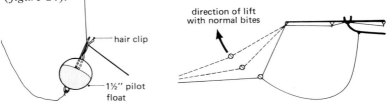

Figure 24

Figure 25

A length of nylon connects the base of the indicator to the front of the rod-rest (*figure 25*). The angler makes his cast, takes up the initial slack, lays his rod down in the rests, walks to the front and clips the bobbin on to the mainline between 10 and 40 inches from the top ring. He then releases a few turns of line from the reel. These turns are taken up and tensioned by the weight of the bobbin. The amount of line released by the angler – and tensioned by the bobbin – is the amount of line that can be taken by a fish before it feels the resistance of the rod.

The doughbobbin method of bite-indication offers:

1. An immediate visual warning of even the most tentative bite.
2. Time for a bite to develop – while the fish takes up the slack.
3. Time for the angler to 'read' the bite.

Although extremely sensitive, the doughbobbin rig has never been popular with the match angler. Fitting it wastes too much time. For this reason, ledgering was largely ignored until the reintroduction of the time-saving swing-tip rig.

Mechanically, the swing-tip and the doughbobbin are the same; but the swing-tip is a time-saver. *Figure 27* and *figure 25* illustrate the similarity between the two systems. *Figure 28* shows the swing-tip in action over a streamy run, and displays the expected tip movement with normal and slack-line baits.

Sometimes this movement will be the merest twitch; at other times a dramatic swing. Delicacy of movement applies more particularly to roach bites – for which the swing-tip was originally designed.

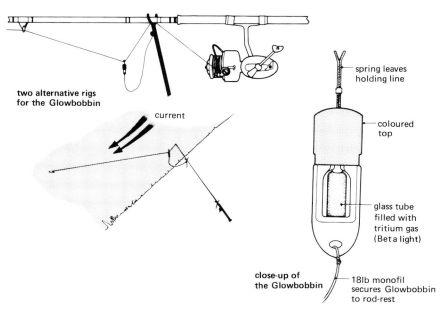

two alternative rigs
for the Glowbobbin

current

spring leaves
holding line

coloured
top

glass tube
filled with
tritium gas
(Beta light)

close-up of
the Glowbobbin

18lb monofil
secures Glowbobbin
to rod-rest

Figure 26   There are two super-modern versions of the doughbobbin, called
the Doughbob *(figure 24)* and the Glowbobbin. They are provided with the
best line-release clip that we have seen. The Doughbob has a screw-capped
body which allows shot to be added, so that an adjustment can be made
for different current strengths. With the Glowbobbin (illustrated here) extra
weighting can be provided by pinching shot on the tethering string

Where bites are expected to take the form of runs taking off many yards
of line, as in carp fishing, a narrow strip of sheet plastic can be folded over
the line between butt ring and reel, and its ends trapped in the clip of the
Glowbobbin

The light element in a glowbobbin consists of what is known as a Beta-
light. This is a tube coated on the inside with a material similar to that used
in television tubes and filled with radioactive tritium gas. (Tritium gas has
an active life of more than twenty years)

Care must be taken when setting up the rod-rest position for
swing-tipping. Swing-tip movement should always be at right angles
to the wind, otherwise the more subtle tweaks (which at times may
be the only bites) will go unnoticed.

When angling in strong winds, take care to shield the swing-tip
and the line. Make the best use of natural cover – if necessary, use
some form of artificial shield. Arrange for the swing-tip to hang near
to the water, since air-currents close to water are usually less turbulent.

Figure 27

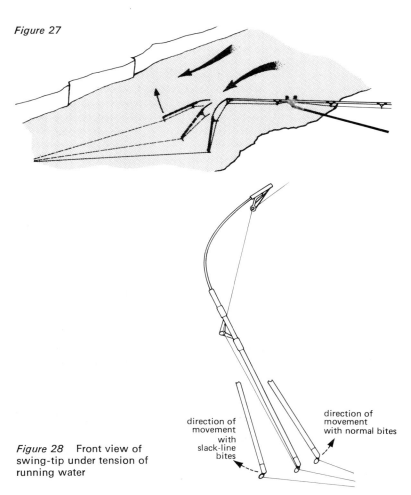

Figure 28 Front view of swing-tip under tension of running water

direction of movement with slack-line bites

direction of movement with normal bites

Although the swing-tip was described in an early nineteenth century book (for details see p. 132) there is no evidence that it was in general use at that time. During the 1960s Jack Clayton reintroduced the swing-tip after which it became very popular – especially with match anglers. We are grateful to Colin Graham for this photograph of Clayton's *original* swing-tip

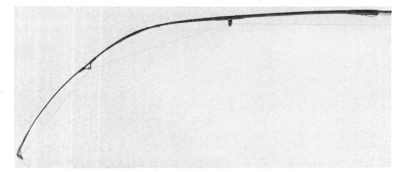

The electric bite-alarm

In 1949 R.W. introduced a very simple electric bite-alarm (made from a bicycle lamp) for the benefit of those carp anglers who fished in the dark. By 1951 he had developed a more sophisticated alarm that incorporated proper relay contacts. In this latter type, the line running between the reel and butt-ring was delicately trapped between sprung electrical contacts thereby separating them and breaking the circuit.

An on/off switch incorporated in the design allowed an angler to cast and set up the alarm in the 'off' position. Once set up and with the switch in the 'on' position the circuit to the buzzer would be completed the moment a fish pulled line away from the contacts. This type of alarm was used by R.W. when he caught the British record rod-caught carp in 1952.

By 1953 he had invented a bite-alarm with a new feature – a spring antenna. This antenna-type alarm has now been in general use for over twenty years and has been used for other species besides carp – particularly bream and tench.

The antenna-type bite-alarm was superior in that unlike previous models which, once activated, had to be switched off manually (at a time when an angler could be fully engaged playing a fish), it stopped as soon as the rod was picked up. Moreover the antenna-type stopped if the fish stopped running or if the fish dropped the bait.

R.W.'s 44 lb record carp was caught in 1952. This photograph was taken when it was alive in the Aquarium at the London Zoo. A scale reading at the time of capture showed the fish to be fifteen years old. When it died in 1971 aged thirty-four its weight was down to 28 lb and its scales showed no evidence of its nineteen years' life in an aquarium

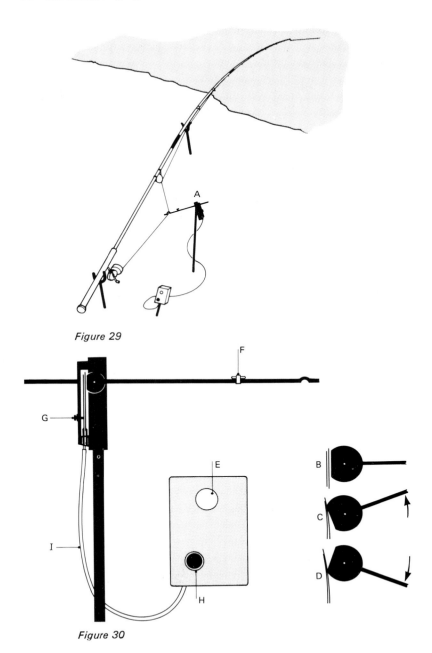

Figure 29

Figure 30

Recently R.W. has again been experimenting with electric bite-alarms and the principles, but not the blueprint, of his latest designs are now illustrated and explained.

When a fish moves an angler's bait it takes or gives line. It can be seen that if an angler uses the layout shown in *figure 29* this taking or giving of line will raise or lower the arm of the bite-alarm pivoting at A.

The raising or lowering of the arm completes an electrical circuit since the cam on the end of the arm causes the contacts (normally separated as in *figure 30* B) to touch as indicated in C and D.

When the circuit is completed a warning light flashes at E and the alarm (buzzer) sounds. A useful extra is the fitting of a Beta light at F. This continuously glowing light will tell an angler fishing in total darkness whether the arm has been raised or lowered – information that will indicate the direction of the fish's movement.

The adjusting screw at G adjusts the sensitivity of the alarm and the push button H is an on/off switch allowing an angler to make all the adjustments during the setting up of the alarm without the attendant flashing and buzzing. I is the cable that connects the buzzer and warning light unit to the cam contact unit (here shown in section to reveal the workings). In practice this unit must be water-proofed – see *figure 31*.

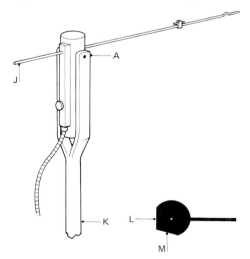

Figure 31

The pivot for the entire head must be on the same axis as that of the cam. This should have quite a bit of friction, so that once set it stays put. In *figures 29* and *31* the axes are at A, but *figure 29* shows how the right angle between the arm and the head is maintained even though the angle between the head and the bankstick has been changed to suit the fishing situation.

J is a handle for tilting the head to the required angle about the bankstick K.

The cam should have a profile with flats at L and M. The second flat ensures that when you've had a bite and struck, and the line has disengaged from the arm, the arm falls to its fullest extent, at which point buzzer and bulb switch off. For the buzzer to keep on sounding when you are into a fish is a major annoyance for some obscure psychological reason.

Touch-ledgering

Touch-ledgering consists of holding the rod in one hand, and the line (between butt-ring and reel) in the fingers of the other, while you are fishing with ledger or paternoster tackle.

The advantages of this method over visual bite-indicators are:

1. It is much more sensitive. Bites that would not register on a visual indicator can be *felt*.
2. It can be used in bad light where 'visual' indicators cannot be seen.
3. It enables an angler to 'read' the nature of the bottom while he moves the end-tackle over the area being fished. This aspect of touch-ledgering is most important, since it is possible, with experience, to tell if the lead is resting on mud, sand, gravel, stones or rock, or whether it is being held up by weed.

An angler experienced in touch-ledgering can soon form a mental picture of the river or lake bed where he is fishing, after which he can allow his tackle to dwell in the areas he thinks most likely to hold fish. He can also concentrate his groundbaiting on these areas, once they have been located.

It is of great advantage to try the method in waters clear enough for the bottom to be seen, so that the sensations produced in the line by the movement of the lead over different sorts of bottom can be more quickly learned.

Indication by touch is the classic method used by the boat angler at sea. He holds the line taut with his finger-tips and feels for the bite. Barbel and chub anglers in particular make use of the same principle and call it touch-ledgering

In order to touch-ledger accurately and well, it is important to be comfortably seated. Let us suppose you are fishing from the left bank of a river and are right-handed. Place your basket or stool so that you sit facing directly across the river. The reel should be attached well up the butt of the rod, so that the part of the rod handle below the reel can be rested on top of the right thigh and held there with the right elbow. If everything is positioned correctly, this alone is sufficient to hold the rod – which allows both hands free for baiting-up or for adjusting the end-tackle. While the bait is in the fishing position, however, the right hand grips the rod at the reel in such a way as to allow either the first or second finger to turn the reel. In the case of a centre-pin, the drum can be turned; if the reel is a fixed-spool, then the finger can turn the pick-up carrier.

The object of this grip is to allow any line pulled in by the fingers of the left hand to be taken up on the reel without your having to change the position of the hands, or having to release line from the left hand to permit it to turn the reel handle. The left hand must operate well in front of the reel, specially when a fixed-spool is used, otherwise the recovered line will be wound where it shouldn't be.

This may sound a slow and inefficient means of recovery, but remember, its purpose is to allow the line to the ledger to be kept taut, and the ledger moved a little from time to time, without altering the sensitive position of the hands holding the rod and the line respectively.

The ledger may be moved by raising the rod somewhat, as well as by left-hand finger movement. In either case, there will be a little slack to take up.

When it is time to wind in, or after a fish is hooked, the left hand releases the line and moves to the reel handle. The right hand stays where it was, ready to apply finger pressure to the drum or spool if necessary.

These measures ensure sensitive control of the tackle and instant knowledge that the bait has been taken, or is being nibbled, by a fish. Experience combined with common sense soon enables the angler to distinguish between bites and line movement caused by wind, swaying weed streamers, floating debris or variation in the current.

There are times when bites are registered by high-frequency vibrations in the line, reminiscent of wind in telephone wires. Barbel are often responsible for such bites, which are undetectable by any other means than touch.

What are known as 'line-bites', indications caused by fish brushing against the line instead of taking the bait, are easily diagnosed by the angler who is touch-ledgering.

Broadly speaking, the slower the current the more difficult touch-ledgering becomes. In running water, the line between ledger and rod-tip is curved, and the pressure of the current on this curve of line keeps sensitive contact, compensating for inadvertent movements on the part of the angler. The slower the current, the more closely the line curve approximates to a straight line and the less is the compensation for accidental movements of the rod by the angler. This means that in very slow or still water, great concentration is needed to avoid the lead moving (when that is not desired) or allowing the line to go slack – when sensitive contact with the tackle is lost.

For this reason, it is sensible for the angler fishing still water to provide himself with an alternative to touch-ledgering. A rod-rest and bite-indicator of the doughbobbin principle, will enable him to relax between spells of touch-ledgering – which can be resumed if bites become frequent.

Commonly in slow or still-water fishing, shoals of tench, bream, roach, rudd and perch tend to move about, so that the angler can expect long spells of inaction interspersed with periods when bites are frequent. During these periods touch-ledgering can be used and advantage taken of the angler's ability to move the bait attractively: this often induces a take from a fish that would have ignored stationary bait.

It must be understood that a high standard of touch-ledgering is not something that is easily understood. Masters of the method have taken as long to reach their present standard as it takes the average violinist to become a professional. It is a method that must be persevered with for many, many fishing hours before full proficiency is attained. Very often in his early stages, the novice will strike at sensations that are not caused by bites, and fail to strike at others that are. But to master the art of touch-ledgering is well worth the time and trouble involved, because once you have passed a certain stage no other means of fishing ledger-tackle can equal it.

Night fishing

Night fishing is probably the most controversial topic among coarse-fish anglers. To some it appears to be little short of poaching; to others it is the most sporting kind of fishing. It has become increasingly popular in recent years and is now allowed on many waters where it was previously banned. But of course it has been practised for a great many years by dedicated anglers who know its difficulties only too well.

From time to time a few voices are raised in protest by people who have never tried it and who think that because they themselves do not practise it, night fishing should be banned. Their arguments are illogical and largely ruled by emotion. Despite what is said to the contrary, night fishing for bream, carp, tench and barbel is demanding of both skill and patience and the angler who imagines that fish give themselves up after dark is living in a dream world.

Nevertheless, in times of low water and hot weather many fish tend to feed better after dark. Where boat traffic, picnickers and swimmers make fishing impossible during the day, night-time offers the only real chance of success. Many anglers have tried it, and gone away disillusioned because they have been unaware of the particular problems involved. A few simple precautions and a little understanding can prevent disillusionment, so for those who are 'in the dark' about night fishing we offer a few words of advice.

First, it is essential to have everything prepared, and to be settled in the swim in daylight. Look it over, cast across it and learn the snags while you can still see them. Put all gear where it can be reached easily and without disturbance. Have a torch handy for use when landing a big fish, but try not to use it for anything else. If you must bait up by torchlight use a shaded pencil torch.

Simple ledger or leadless tackle is the most suitable rig for night fishing. After casting, some form of bite-indicator should be attached to the line between the first two butt-rings. This can be anything from a simple fold of silver paper to a sophisticated electric bite-alarm; but whatever the choice, it should be attached so that the line can run freely once a fish takes the bait. An indicator that jams in the rod rings or causes the line to tighten against a biting fish is of little value at night when big fish are likely to be hooked.

At night, tackle can be stronger, and hooks and baits larger than in daylight. Bites are usually bolder, because fish tend to take baits with more confidence after dark.

In rivers, especially where the current is strong, it will probably be impossible to fit any kind of bite-detector. In these circumstances it is necessary to hold the rod and feel for a bite. Usually there is no mistaking them and fewer will be missed if the rod is already in the hand.

Night fishing can be cold and comfortless if conditions are bad, so take a comfortable seat – a deck-chair if possible – and a big angler's umbrella. Wear warm clothing and always take a couple of flasks of hot drink – spiked or otherwise according to taste – to sustain you through the night.

5 Floats and Float Fishing

Design and application

In considering float design, the emphasis has always been on buoyancy; other important matters tend to be neglected.

It is clearly important that a float should be buoyant, otherwise it is not a float. In some circumstances there is great advantage in making floats from the most buoyant materials available, so as to keep shot weight high compared to float weight. If the shot weighs more than the float, it will travel ahead of the float when the tackle is cast, promoting more accurate casting and avoiding any tendency for the tackle to tangle in the air. This is what we want in most kinds of fishing, but not in all.

If it is desired to fish very close to an opposite bank, or to overhanging branches, or a bed of rushes or reeds towards which the angler can cast, it is preferable to use a float that is heavier than the shot it carries. The float will then travel ahead of the shot. It can be cast very close to the far bank, or the reeds. The sinking shot will swing down below it. This effect can be obtained with floats made of buoyant materials, by placing some of the shot very close to the float; but in such a case the buoyancy of the float offers no advantages, and the float will be larger and have greater air and water resistance than a heavier float.

Float sensitivity is commonly regarded as a matter of residual buoyancy. Unfortunately there are other factors involved.

Let us consider a typical antenna float consisting of a balsa-wood body on a thin cane stem. The float is loaded with shot until all of its body is submerged, and only the antenna projects above the surface of the water. Floats of this kind can be made large or small; the larger they are, the more shot they will carry, but provided they are all shotted to the same level, with all the body under water; and

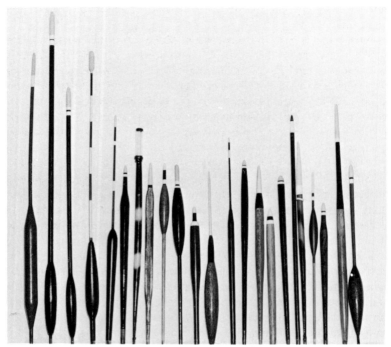

Float patterns are legion. This photograph shows a representative range of modern floats – excluding pike floats.

provided all have antennae of the same diameter, then their residual buoyancy will be exactly the same, regardless of their size and the weight of shot they will carry. The addition of an extra small shot will take all of them deeper by the same amount.

This leads many anglers to suppose that all are therefore equally sensitive. This is not the case, because as well as residual buoyancy we have also to consider water resistance and inertia. The bigger the float and the more shot there are on the line, the greater the water resistance when the tackle is moved by a biting fish. The heavier the float and its load of shot, the greater is the inertia of the tackle. It takes force to move a mass from rest. It takes force to overcome water resistance.

You can confirm this by a very simple experiment. Take a couple of floats of similar design but of which one is much bigger, and able to carry more shot, than the other. Put the smaller float on your line and pinch on just enough shot to take it under water. Cast it out and let it sink.

Now wind it in at various speeds. Make a series of casts, so that you get the feel of how hard it is to start it moving and keep it moving through the water. Having done so, change to the bigger float and again pinch on just enough shot to take it under. Repeat what you did with the smaller float. You will easily discover how much extra effort is needed to start that bigger float moving, because of its greater inertia; and to keep it moving through the water, because of its greater water resistance.

Remember that in order to signal a bite – except in the case of a 'lift' bite – a fish has to move the float and keep it moving. Now you will realize why you should use the smallest float and lightest shotting that you can, having regard to the requirements of the distance you have to cast, and the need for good control when the tackle is in the water.

Inertia is proportional to the weight of the tackle, but water resistance depends mainly on the shape of the float. If you want to investigate this, try making a float whose body consists of a thin flat cork disc set on a stem so that it looks like a coin with a nail driven through its centre. Attach your line via rubber tubes at each end of the stem and try pulling that float through the water. You will find the water resistance enormous by comparison with a float able to carry exactly the same shot load, but having a very slim body. So, generally speaking, a long slim body for a float is preferable to a short fat one. It offers far less water resistance to a biting fish.

The actual shape of the body matters, too. Ideally, the greatest diameter ought to be about a third of the way back from the front end; when a float is being pulled down by a fish, the bottom end is the front end. That is also the best shape for travelling through the air when you cast, when again, the bottom of the float is the front end. A correctly shaped float is best able to fly through the air without tumbling end over end and tangling the tackle.

There are, however, circumstances in which some degree of water resistance greater than what is ideal has to be tolerated, as when one is fishing turbulent water, for which floats of more or less egg-shape may be needed; slim floats being prone to being drawn under by vortices and miniature whirlpools.

However efficient for casting, and sensitive to bites, a float may be, it is of little use if it cannot be seen, except of course when a fish is responsible for its temporary invisibility; H. T. Sheringham once described a favourite float as 'pleasing in appearance and even more pleasing in disappearance'. The visibility of a float depends upon a number of factors; among them are colour in relation to background, and size of the visible part in relation to the distance at which the float is viewed.

Obviously, a light-coloured float-top is easiest to see against a dark surface, while a dark top shows up best against the reflection of white clouds or blue sky. Black is too readily confused with other floating objects if used alone. Red looks black at more than a few yards' distance. Very often the surface is broken by ripple, giving a light and dark dappled effect; or a float may pass from a part of the surface that reflects sky, to one reflecting dark trees. Consequently a good all-round colour for a float-top is daylight fluorescent light orange at the extreme tip, followed by a white band, followed in turn by a black band which may in fact consist of the line-retaining cap.

The thinner the top of the float, the less is its residual buoyancy, but the more difficult it is to see, and the less is the distance at which it can be seen. Such sensitivity as is obtained by low residual buoyancy need not be sacrificed to any great extent if the top of the float is of cruciform section, like very abbreviated dart flights, which have little residual buoyancy but plenty of visible area. Such a top also serves to stabilize the flight of the float through the air in casting.

It remains to remark on the value of floats having fluted bodies for long-trotting in running water. Such floats have low water resistance to pulls in line with the float, but high resistance to pulls at right angles. This makes it easier to keep the line between float and rod-top free from too many curves and bends, with the float's progress downstream being seriously checked. Fluted floats have no advantage except for long-trotting, though as we have said a fluted *tip* on a normal float increases visibility without greatly increasing buoyancy.

There can be no disadvantage, and there may be some advantage, in painting or staining the underwater portions of floats in a brown, olive or green colour to match natural objects in the water.

Nowadays, so many different types of float are available in the shops that many anglers are confused about which to choose. In practice, an angler having a range of bird-quill floats from crow through goose and turkey to swan, with a few lengths of peacock quill, will need to add only a few balsa-and-cane antenna floats to be equipped for most kinds of float fishing. For pike, long narrow celluloid floats with hollow central tubes are very good and can be used fixed or sliding.

Few anglers appreciate the technical differences between floats in the wide range available today.

Fashions develop. Someone designs a float for a specialized form of fishing, uses it, wins a contest or catches a lot of fish, and that float becomes the 'in' float for the season. The result is that this particular design is used in situations that are completely unsuited to it; consequently, of course, it doesn't work. For instance, when fluted floats were enjoying a period of popularity someone had the notion of making an *antenna* float with a fluted body! Just about the daftest float you could imagine. The fluted float is used for trotting, it is designed so that the current *pushes* it on its way. The antenna float is designed for still water, to sit with the body submerged so that it rides the waves and avoids the wind. Basically, these two floats are utterly different; any attempt to marry them is absurd. The result simply adds one more attractive (but comparatively useless) float to an already overcrowded box!

3 lb 14 oz Roach. The one-time record caught by W. Penney while fishing Molesey Reservoir on 6 September 1938

It is fun making floats and there are all sorts of materials which lend themselves to the production of special creations. But although many of these floats are attractive, and undoubtedly give their users a lot of pleasure, the materials used are often of the wrong kind.

There are very few materials that have the properties essential to good float-making.

The two main functions of a float are:

1. The presentation of the bait.
2. The registration of bites.

To achieve both these ends a float needs two special properties: lightness and buoyancy. The importance of lightness and buoyancy in floats is not generally understood, and because of this the particular functions of specialized floats are seldom fully grasped.

If, for example, you consider the uses of a trotting float and think of the basic shape, it is obvious that the most buoyant part of the float is at the top end near the surface of the water. This is because the float has to be stable and ride steadily in a strong current. Those swirly eddies that build up in fast-flowing rivers tend to suck an unstable float under; so, sufficient of the thick end of the float has to be above the water-line to prevent it.

If you took the same float, turned it upside down and shotted it so that only an inch of the thin end protruded above the water, it would be sucked under. It is the same float, but its buoyancy has now been transferred to the *bottom* end, and as a trotting float, it is no longer practical. (It is, of course, possible to reverse the float using the *same amount of shot* and achieve the same result, but in practice the float becomes very unstable.)

There are three points to remember about trotting floats:

1. They are buoyant because they are big and light.
2. They are designed to carry quite a lot of shot because a lot of shot is needed to get the bait down in fast water.
3. They have good fat tips, which remain visible.

Let us look at a few floats and their special application.

Some finer points of float fishing in running water

Trotting float tackle in running water is usually done with either a centre-pin or a fixed-spool reel. The method of using and controlling the centre-pin is well known and there is no need to describe it here. The procedure when the fixed-spool reel is used does need some explanation.

Ideally a fixed-spool reel should have the following features, assuming the angler is right-handed:

1. The handle should be on the left-hand side.
2. The pick-up carrier ('bowl' or 'flyer') should rotate, when winding in, in a clockwise direction as viewed from the front of the spool.
3. The pick-up, if automatic, should trip at such a point that it does not rap the angler's index finger when this is touching the spool.
4. The pick-up guide should preferably incorporate a rotating roller.
5. The reel should be so designed that the index finger of the right hand can easily reach the front lip of the spool, when the rod is being held comfortably.

Such important attributes as smooth gearing, a reliable slipping clutch and a comfortable handle, are required in any fixed-spool reel but the five points given above are specially important for long-trotting.

Let us now assume that a right-handed angler is ready to start fishing. Having adjusted his tackle correctly and baited the hook, he casts out in the usual way, but instead of engaging the pick-up, he traps the line against the front lip of the spool with the index finger of the right hand. This prevents any more line from being released.

He raises the rod-point and checks the float for such time as he judges will be needed to allow the shot to sink. Exactly how much checking can be done without causing the float to swing in towards the near bank, will depend on the loading of the tackle and the speed of the current. In general the float ought not to travel more than a foot or two downstream before the shots have sunk; the angler knows when they have, because the float will cock.

If it proves impossible to hold the float until it cocks without it swinging into the near bank too much, or travelling too far downstream, it will be necessary to change to a larger float that carries a heavier load of shot.

In a deep, fast swim on rivers such as the Hampshire Avon or the Herefordshire Wye, a float large enough to carry four or five swan shot may be needed. On a slow swim on the Great Ouse or parts of the Thames, a float that cocks with a single BB shot might suffice. It

English trotting tackle proved effective for the big rainbows of Silver Creek, Idaho, USA, where method is not restricted — note the large landing net

is important to have the right combination of float and shot for the swim one has chosen to fish; without it proper tackle control is difficult, if not impossible.

Having checked the float to allow the shot to sink, check it for another half-second and then allow it to travel on its way downstream by letting coils of line slip from under the controlling forefinger. There are two ways of doing this. Either the line can be allowed to slip continuously, or the rod can be raised simultaneously with several feet of line being released; after which the forefinger is pressed on to the spool lip and the rod-point lowered to allow the float to proceed. By repeating this process, the float is worked downstream as far as is thought desirable.

As it travels, the line between it and the rod-point must be kept under control and not allowed to lie in a large curve, or in a series of curves. The variations in surface currents, and sometimes the effects of wind, will result in the line being anything but straight to the float, if paid off completely freely. It is never possible to achieve a perfectly straight line between rod and float, but by checking it with the forefinger and lifting the rod-point, the line can be partially straightened before the float's progress is noticeably affected. A float with a fluted body, which offers greater resistance to a pull at right-angles to its long axis but no more resistance to a biting fish, helps the task of keeping the line straighter.

The act of checking the line at the spool and raising the rod will lift a good deal of the line off the water, then by moving the rod-point left or right before lowering it, the line can be laid on the water in such a way as to compensate for the effects of wind and current. If for example the tendency is for the line to belly downstream, it can be lifted and laid down farther upstream. If it tends to lag too far behind the float, perhaps due to the effects of a back-eddy, it can be lifted and laid farther downstream.

It is important to understand that the angler is constantly busy, not only in controlling the rate of pay-off from the reel but also in keeping the line between rod-tip and float under control. At the same time he has to concentrate on his float as it travels.

Holding back the float to the extent that it lies at an angle to the surface, and causes a 'V'-shaped pattern at the surface, is wrong, except when done deliberately to cause the bait to rise in the water. When the bait is maggot, or caddis, or if an artificial shrimp or nymph is being fished on, a deliberate severe check of the float can induce a bite. Otherwise it is better to apply very little checking, so that the bait travels at the natural speed of the current near the bottom, vertically below the float or a little behind it.

Upon seeing an indication of a bite, the angler drops the forefinger of his right hand to the front lip of the reel spool and traps the line, and the rod is raised smartly to tighten on the fish. If the fish is hooked, the forefinger is drawn up towards the rod, taking the line with it. This is why it is important to use a reel having the correct direction of rotation, clockwise as you look at the outer face of the spool. The line is caught against the ball of the forefinger and as that finger is crooked, slides into the crease where the end joint of the finger joins the second joint. The line to the fish is now taut. The left hand turns the reel handle; the pick-up trips and, as it comes round, neatly removes the line from the forefinger. There is no slackening of the line at this critical moment. This is very important because, contrary to common belief, a hook is seldom pulled in over its barb by the act of striking or tightening. It works its way in during the first thirty seconds or so after the initial connection is made. Consequently, if the pull of the line on the hook is momentarily slackened during this time, the hook is very likely to come away from the fish.

It is possible to engage the pick-up before tightening, but this inevitably means relinquishing control by the forefinger and several coils of line can slip from the spool. Not only is there a time delay, but also, and especially in windy conditions, these loose coils can catch round the pick-up and lead to a break if the hooked fish is a big one. The break may well take place at the reel, with the consequent loss of the end tackle and a lot of line.

Catching the line on the forefinger, and taking it off that finger with the engaged pick-up, is therefore the better method. It is of course necessary, as stated earlier, that the pick-up should trip in the right place relative to the index finger, otherwise the finger receives a severe rap from the bail-arm.

When the fish is hooked, it may be desirable to take advantage of the pause that usually occurs, before the fish realizes it is in trouble, to apply quite a strong pull to bring the head of the fish upstream. If it then bolts, it will move in an upstream direction, and can often be kept moving in that desirable direction by winding, while maintaining considerable pressure. Herein lies the advantage of a rotating roller in the pick-up guide: low friction at this point greatly increases the pressure that can be maintained while winding, without the clutch slipping.

In swims with weed or rushes on one or both sides, the ability to get a big fish headed upstream, and to keep it coming up under heavy pressure while recovering line, is of great value in preventing the fish from turning to one side or the other and getting into the weeds.

In the subsequent proceedings there is a choice of method. Either the clutch of the reel is set to give line when the fish decides to make a run or the handle of the reel can be released, with the clutch kept at a very tight setting.

If a fish makes a series of very long runs against the clutch, followed by line recovery by the angler, as many twists are put into the line as the number of times the spool has rotated. Take as an example a powerful fish whose successive runs add up to 100 yards. That will produce about 400 twists in the line, with a fixed-spool reel of average spool diameter. It would not take many such fish to produce a severe kink problem. There is thus a good case for allowing a fish to take line by releasing the reel handle and allowing the pick-up

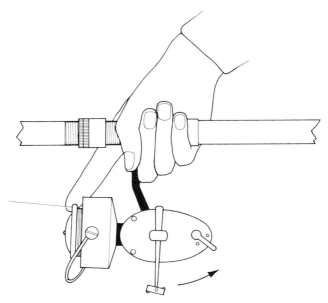

Figure 32   The common method of playing a fish on a fixed-spool reel
is by means of a lightly set clutch and finger pressure on the spool lip.
The reel handle is *only* wound when line can be retrieved — never against a
running fish.

Figure 33   Although a slipping clutch is incorporated in almost every
fixed-spool reel, some anglers (F.B. among the authors) much prefer to
give line to a running fish by releasing the handle and allowing it to rotate
backwards. During a run the bowl or pick-up-carrier also rotates backwards
allowing an angler to apply the appropriate finger pressure.

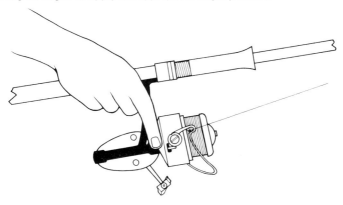

carrier to rotate backwards. This does however have the drawback of needing a reel designed so that a finger can touch the rear of the pick-up carrier to prevent its overrunning when the fish stops, otherwise a dangerous tangle may occur.

When using this latter method, applying a finger to the pick-up carrier is the only means the angler has of varying pressure on a running fish. There is no assistance from the clutch, as there would be if the reel handle were held and the fish allowed to take line by rotating the spool. Clearly, there is a case for designing a fixed-spool reel with a star-drag between the handle and the driving gear, as in multiplier reels, instead of having a clutch in the spool. In practice, however, few fish make enough long runs to cause problems of kink in the line; and it is debatable, therefore, which of the two methods is the better with the reels currently available.

Special floats and their uses

The Trotter

The simple trotting-float or trotter is one of the most widely used and effective floats in the coarse-fisherman's armoury. Its use is generally restricted to moving water but it can be adapted, in the larger sizes, for livebaiting with minnows in still water. Its top buoyancy allows it to support such baits (with suitable adjustments to the shotting) effectively in lakes, and the fact that it is affected by wind drift and surface drag is no disadvantage in this particular instance.

It is in moving water, however, that the trotter really excels and the fishing technique involved is based purely and simply on sending the bait through the chosen stretch of water at the *right depth and speed*. In most cases the right speed is the same as that of the current which presents the bait naturally to the fish. This can sometimes be achieved only by holding back the float slightly so as to slow down the bait's progress in keeping with the speed of the loose feed or groundbait. It is not always necessary to hold back, however. There are times when circumstances do not permit it, and others when it would be unwise to do so, but in most uncomplicated circumstances the trotter can be manipulated to present the bait very naturally. The ideal situation would be a swim with the flow proceeding directly away from the angler and where direct control could be applied from *behind*. A punt anchored at midstream would give such a situation and in this case the tackle would need only to be *dropped in* and allowed to proceed downstream. A spot where the current strikes the near bank and then sets *diagonally across* the river provides another ideal situation for this kind of fishing, but alas such swims are few and far between.

Most river situations call for casting and controlling the tackle from a point at right-angles to the water, and it is here that the technique becomes less simple.

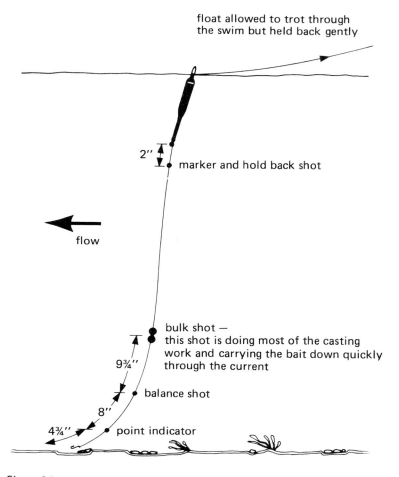

float allowed to trot through
the swim but held back gently

2" marker and hold back shot

flow

bulk shot —
this shot is doing most of the casting
work and carrying the bait down quickly
through the current

9¾"

balance shot

8"

4¾" point indicator

Figure 34   Trotter

J. H. R. Bazley of Leeds, probably the greatest match fisherman of all time, is seen here 'trotting' with a single-action revolving-drum reel. This picture was taken in 1926 at Naburn during the 'All England'

Fishing close to the near bank presents no problem. The rod can be extended over the water, the float held back if necessary and the bait coaxed into position with a minimum of effort. A comparatively small trotter can be used and the shotting shown is ideal for this situation. Quite turbulent water can be fished in this manner without the float deviating from its course, but when it becomes necessary to fish at longer range, two rod-lengths out for instance, a bigger float is called for. The same pattern will still serve but because it is vital to keep the float on an even course at the *right speed* by bending and manipulating the line, it must be bigger. Obviously the bigger float will remain more stable against these line manipulations than a smaller one.

An important consideration at this stage is that line thickness affects the float's behaviour and that, all other things being equal, a line of, say, 5 lb BS would require a bigger float than one of 2 lb.

Used correctly, simple trotting tackle is as good as any, and better than most, for presenting a bait naturally to the fish. Very occasionally, when everything is right, the float will do all the work unassisted once it has been cast, but generally speaking the angler has to *make it behave.*

If the float is pulled off course by yards of unmanageable line, surface drag or by wind, the presentation of the bait will not be natural. Fish will become suspicious. In extreme cases they may *not even see* the bait if it has been allowed to race through too quickly, at the wrong depth, or badly off-course.

Where the bottom is uneven, shallow 'humps' can be negotiated by holding back the float so that the tackle rides clear. Occasionally the very act of causing the bait to rise in the water induces a bite.

The trotter, in its several sizes, is a versatile float, able to accommodate baits as small as hempseed and as large as lob-worms.

Its top buoyancy and top-and-bottom line attachment (as shown) make it an ideal float for most simple river situations, but its extreme lightness and buoyancy stem largely from the fact that it is a one-piece float made of high grade balsa – which is very fragile. A tight-fitting top float cap is necessary to maintain the correct depth setting, but this should always be removed after fishing to prevent grooving under pressure.

The shotting pattern shown will suit most situations but it may sometimes be found necessary to move the bottom point indicator nearer to the hook for improved bite registration.

There are times, too, when it may be advantageous to slide the bulk shot up nearer to the marker. Holding back hard and slowing down the bait's progress when fishing immediately below the rod-tip is a case in point. This, coupled with a raising of the float so that the tackle is set a foot over-depth, is often an effective way of inducing bites.

The top shot helps stabilize the trotter against the actions of line mending and holding back, and it also serves as a marker or guide when the depth setting has to be altered. The trotter, incidentally, functions best in depths between 3 and 7 ft, but is manageable up to 10 ft. Its main disadvantage is that it is virtually useless in a downstream wind.

The Shot-dragger

There are times when fish, for some reason, refuse to take a bait either trotted through at normal speed or anchored hard on the bottom on ledger tackle. We don't know *why*, but we *do* know *how* to tackle the situation and we employ the shot-dragger for the purpose.

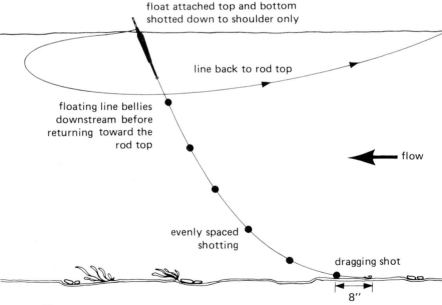

Figure 35   Shot-dragger

The object is to present the bait so that it drags along the bottom slowly, and it will be seen from the diagram that in this particular situation, unlike some others, the float precedes the bait downstream. This is an exceptionally good presentation for barbel, and occasionally for chub and big roach. Bite registration can be confusing at first as the dragging shot often makes the float produce 'false' bites, but experience will quickly distinguish between these and the real ones when they come.

The float is loaded by spacing shots at regular intervals to a position about 8 inches from the hook and these should be sufficient to cock the float to its second shoulder. Then an extra shot is added 8 inches from the hook. This is the one that drags and slows down the progress of the bait. Its size depends on the smoothness of the bottom, and the amount of slowing-down required. Obviously a big shot will slow down the bait's progress more than a small one, and, where the bottom is uneven, complete stoppages are likely to be commonplace. With the right size of dragging shot, however, steady progress can be maintained.

It will be seen from the diagram that the shot-dragger is attached top-and-bottom, and that line comes away from the shoulder in a belly downstream. This belly helps pull the float and tackle downstream against the resistance of the dragging shot but, in the event of a complete stoppage, it is only necessary to lift the rod briefly to start the tackle flowing again. This lifting of the rod, although obviously made in an *upstream* direction, has the effect of increasing the pull on the float *downstream*. The size of the belly, to some extent, controls the drag speed, i.e. the bigger the belly the faster, generally speaking, the float will proceed. But this only applies within certain limits. Obviously too big a belly will render the tackle uncontrollable and make positive striking difficult if not impossible.

Evenly spaced shotting produces a nice fluid curve and holds the float at a steady angle (as shown in the diagram). The line between the float and the rod-tip should be kept greased to ensure best results and line strength should not exceed 5 lb BS.

The shot-dragger fishes best over a clean, even bottom in a steady current and can only be used to real effect in depths no greater than the rod's length. The float should, of course, be set well over depth.

The shot-dragger has one other, though probably less known, application. It can be used very occasionally in still waters where the bottom is free of weed by making use of an offshore or cross wind. (In most situations drift of this kind is regarded as a disadvantage but there are times when otherwise disinterested fish can be stimulated by slight bait movement.)

The dragging technique can only be used in water up to around 10 ft deep, but works equally well on soft mud or hard gravel. The size of the dragging shot obviously depends upon the strength of the wind. In very rough conditions, and when the wind is blowing *towards* the bank, the method is impracticable, but when the surface is rippled or only slightly rippled it can be extremely effective. For some reason small baits such as single maggots or casters seem to produce the best results, but small red worms are often deadly for perch (and trout where permissible).

The Ducker

Although the ducker is a fairly versatile float which can be used in still and running water, its main purpose is to combat a downstream wind.

Its buoyancy is at the bottom and the line attachment must be at the bottom end only. The reason for this is obvious. In order to compete with a downstream wind, which will always push a top-bodied float downstream much too quickly, it is necessary to sink the line, and to have as little of the float exposed to the wind as possible. The ducker, with its bulbous body buried beneath the surface and the line coming away from the bottom end, sails downstream at a natural pace, unaffected by the angler. It tends to look after itself very well without help and there is no need for mending or holding back on the angler's part.

Bottom-end-only float attachments are not widely understood, nor are they used as often as they should be, and it is worthwhile demonstrating, here and now, the various attachments. These apply not only to duckers but to other floats as well, and particularly to still-water floats. Method of attachment is a matter of personal choice. For a downstream wind situation it could be any one of the three illustrated, but for critical depth settings in still waters, the swinger attachment probably serves best.

To ensure that the line sinks quickly after casting, it is advisable to over-cast slightly, sink the rod-tip and wind the float back into the chosen or baited area.

Where speed is important, 'back shotting' with a dust shot pinched on 6–12 inches *behind* the float (i.e. between the float and rod-tip) provides a useful means of sinking the line. Do not use this method in still waters, however, as the back shot will continue to sink after the float has settled. Remember too, that the ducker is used as a fixed float and that it will not function well, nor is it likely to be very manageable, in depths greater than the rod's length.

The ducker can often be used to good effect for trotting at longer range, i.e. two or three rod-lengths out irrespective of wind conditions. There is a critical distance (which obviously varies from time to time) at which a trotter or top-buoyancy float becomes uncontrollable and the ducker takes over, but only practical experience can tell you exactly what this distance is. The shotting pattern for the ducker is fairly standard and the one shown is highly satisfactory.

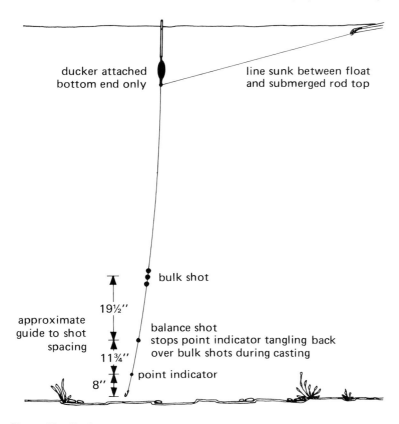

ducker attached bottom end only

line sunk between float and submerged rod top

bulk shot

approximate guide to shot spacing

19½''

11¾''

8''

balance shot
stops point indicator tangling back over bulk shots during casting

point indicator

Figure 36   Ducker

The bottom shot should not be allowed to touch bottom. Let the bait drag by all means if it is considered necessary but keep the important point indicator clear.

Of the four different-sized duckers, the two smallest will fish well on lines *below* 4 lb BS. The two largest may be used on lines of 5 lb and 6 lb respectively, but these strengths should be regarded as the absolute upper limit.

Despite its versatility, the ducker cannot be used in very fast and turbulent water. Its design is such that it is continually pulled under in these conditions and its use should be restricted to rivers of slow and moderate flow.

It is, however, an extremely good float for long-range fishing in shallow lakes, and, because it can be cast 35–40 yards, it is especially useful for far-bank fishing on wide rivers.

The Wire Avon

The wire Avon, a greatly improved version of the earlier cane-stemmed Avon, is a specialist float with strictly limited capabilities, but, when used within the bounds of its limitations, it is the perfect float. In order to define the wire Avon's narrow limitations, it may be advisable to record immediately the circumstances in which it will *not* function – and these, at first glance, appear to be a formidable list.

The wire Avon should not be used in a downstream wind, in a turbulent current, in still water, or at long range. It should not be used with big baits, heavy lines or in deep water, and it should not be used with a bottom-end-only line attachment.

So where and how can it be used, and what are its special advantages?

The wire Avon is a trotting float for use in rivers of medium-to-fast flow which are not too wide or too deep. For lively little rivers averaging 20 to 30 ft wide, and ranging in depth from 3 to 8 ft, it is the ideal float. Used in conjunction with fine lines, small hooks, small particle baits, and similar loose feed, it can achieve perfect presentation. Lines of from 1 to 3 lb BS are suited to the wire Avon's special function – that of trotting through, precisely 'on depth', as illustrated in the shotting diagram.

If the loose feed has been introduced in the correct quantity and in the right spot upstream, there will be many identical particles of food passing through the swim very close to, and occasionally bumping along, the bottom. The hookbait has to behave in exactly the same manner and travel at the same speed. It has to appear to be as unattached as the 'free offerings', and good float control is needed to achieve this. It may be necessary to hold back briefly, or for a fairly long period.

It may be necessary to hold back very lightly in order to check the bait's progress only slightly, or it may be necessary to hold back hard to make the bait rise attractively in the water. (Small current fluctuations often do this to the loose particles, and it has already been established that the act of holding back sometimes induces bites.)

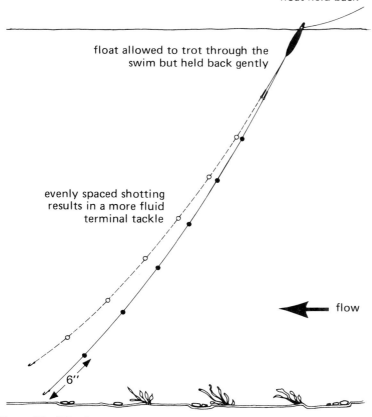

float held back

float allowed to trot through the
swim but held back gently

evenly spaced shotting
results in a more fluid
terminal tackle

flow

6"

Figure 37   Wire Avon

The even shotting pattern shown is the most suitable for the wire Avon because it is fluid and easily controlled at short range. It is not the best pattern for long casting as it is more prone to tangling than bunched shotting, but in these particular circumstances no long casts are ever likely to be required. The wire stem acts rather like a keel in that it holds the float stable. It allows it to be checked without being pulled off course, and without being made to lie flat on the surface, in which position bites are less likely to be recognized.

Even against hard checking the wire Avon tends to sit more or less upright because of the wire stem's stability.

If it is considered necessary to let the bait trip bottom, the float may be set over depth, but only the bait should be allowed to touch bottom. The end shot should always ride clear, and some slight adjustment may be required here from time to time, depending upon the size and nature of the bait.

Laying-on

When fish show more inclination to feed on the bottom, as they do sometimes in colder weather (or where there is an easily exploited source of food lying on the bottom in the form of a groundbait carpet), it is logical to present the bait there. Laying-on simply means that the bait is placed on the bottom and held there by a shot or shots heavy enough to overcome the effects of drift or current.

Regular trotting tackle can usually be adapted for laying-on by setting the tackle deeper and sliding extra shot down towards the hook.

In the case of a two-shot slimline float being used in calm, still water, or in a very slow-moving current, it means that both shots should be bulked close together near the hook. The distance between the hook and shot is a matter for personal choice and depends upon the bait being used and the nature of the bites. A buoyant crust bait, for instance, would normally be fished very close to the anchoring shots in order to keep it down on the bottom. Soft crust is quickly sucked off the hook by a biting fish and close shotting obviously helps register bites more quickly. Big baits such as paste or lobworms may be fished on a longer 'trail' (the term used to describe the length of link between hook and shots) and 12 to 18 inches is not an uncommon length. Bites are usually positive in this situation and there is no real need for instant registration on the float.

Heavier float tackle in faster water may be set for laying-on in similar fashion, i.e. the float is set deeper and extra shots are placed nearer the hook. Stringing out the bulk shots may help prevent bowing in the line when the current is very fast.

The float lies at half-cock when the bait is 'laid-on' and it usually settles close in to the near bank out of the main stream. Holding the rod out over the water and adjusting the shotting accordingly will allow the faster water farther out to be fished.

Laying-on can be practised at long range in still waters by using specialized floats which are streamlined, have great shot-carrying capacity (to achieve distance) and an ability to remain stable in all but the strongest wind.

These floats are usually attached at the bottom end only, in order that the first few feet of line are sunk below the surface, and though the baits are still laid-on these floats do not lie at half-cock in the traditional (and not particularly efficient) style.

Using these specialized floats to fish at long range in windy conditions is very close to lift-fishing and in many cases the bite will only be registered by the float rising slowly and positively in the water when the anchoring shots are moved from the bottom.

Stret-pegging

Holding back a trotting tackle to clear an occasional obstruction on the bottom sometimes causes the bait to rise up in the water in a manner attractive to fish. Stret-pegging was possibly developed because of this discovery. The method is old and well established, though there is no indication as to how its name is derived.

Stret-pegging, or stretting as it is often called, is a method used in near-bank swims and is particularly effective in flood water. The tackle is set deeper than the water and is allowed to settle briefly downstream after casting. Then the rod is lifted, a yard or so more line is paid out, and the tackle allowed to settle again. The procedure is repeated until the maximum downstream area has been exploited, at which stage the tackle is re-cast. It is really a combination of near-bank trotting and laying-on tactics; its effectiveness lies in the fact that it covers a big area of water at all depths – slowly and methodically. While the rod-point is being lifted, the tackle rises from the bottom and the bait may even show briefly on the surface. A bite could come at any depth. While the rod is in the rest, where it normally stays between moves, the bait spends most of its time on the

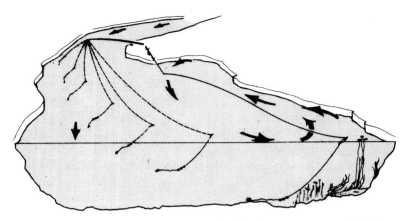

Figure 38 A section through a stream showing how a stret-pegged float rig sweeps from the far bank to the nearside bank

bottom, but it is subjected to sideways movements as the peculiarities of the current sweep the float out from the bank and back again. From the bank to several feet out the water is therefore covered effectively throughout the whole length of the swim *at all depths*.

The float lies at half-cock when resting and throughout the whole time the line is usually taut from bait to rod-tip.

Bites may be registered by the float moving sideways (difficult to recognize at times), lying flat, or diving under so that the rod-tip bends towards the water.

Aspects of Lift-fishing

Most anglers regard the 'lift' style of float fishing as one that was designed exclusively for tench fishing. It is true that, of recent years, it has been used more and more to deal with shy biting tench in summer, but its application certainly doesn't end there. It can be used in winter as well as in summer and for a large variety of other coarse fish. For instance F.J.T. enjoys catching rudd in winter and is surprised that more anglers do not set out to catch them then. They provide a good second string to livebaiting or deadbaiting for pike and they respond extremely well to lift-fishing.

Lift-fishing has seen many changes during the past ten years or so but before we go into details, it should be explained that the old-style lift rig was especially suited to still-water fishing. It comprised a

7 lb Tench. The one-time record tench caught by the Rev. E. C. Alston while fishing Ringmere in Norfolk on 8 July 1933

short length of peacock quill which was attached to the line at the bottom end only, by means of a wide, tight-fitting float cap.

There are several points to remember about lift floats made of peacock quill, and the most important ones are:

1. They should be cocked by one shot pinched on near the hook.
2. The tackle should be set deeper than the water.
3. The line should be drawn taut till the float cocks and then left that way.

The rod remains in a rest the whole time and the strike is made from the rod-rest. Generally speaking this rig, scaled up or down depending upon the circumstances, will deal with finicky bites from good-quality fish in still water. It will not work in a fast stream, though it can be put to good use in rivers with a slow current. Its effectiveness lies in its ability to present a bait on the bottom, with an immediate response to quick bites. The fact that the shot is near to the bait means that a good fish cannot move the bait without moving the shot too, and the moment the shot is dislodged from the bottom the float rises in the water and lies flat.

Technically, of course, this float has a number of disadvantages. It is neither very buoyant nor very versatile. It reacts nicely to the bite of a fish, but because of its shape and modest buoyancy its movements are sometimes very quick, which means that the angler has to be 'quick on the draw'.

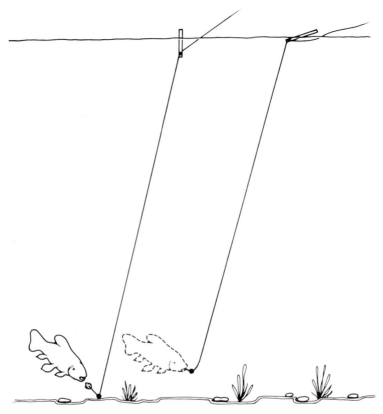

Figure 39 Simple peacock-quill lift-tackle in action. The bait is literally sucked in by the fish, the bottom anchor shot is dislodged, the float lifts and lies flat on the surface. In critical situations it is necessary to strike while the 'lift' is in progress

Today there are more sophisticated floats, and the 'windbeater' type, with its long antenna and very buoyant sight-bulb, is an improvement on the simple quill. Shotting such a float is a precise operation but once the correct loading has been established the whole rig remains very stable and sensitive. These floats are some 15 inches long and are shotted down so that only the buoyant sight-bulb remains above water. This is achieved by loading the terminal tackle with suspended shots until the main body of the float is submerged. The antenna is then taken down by the weight of one tiny shot which rests on the bottom. If the bait is a heavy one – e.g. a lobworm – it will be sufficient to take the antenna down, and the small shot can be dispensed with. This rig will fish in the strongest of winds and remain stable in very rough water because so little of the float is exposed. Bites are almost invariably registered by a lift and keeling over of the float. The whole set-up, fully explained in the next section, is extremely sensitive.

This sensitivity is especially important for winter rudd fishing, for although rudd are often bold biters in summer, they can be extremely finicky in winter. They do, however, often respond quite well to moderate groundbaiting in reasonable conditions. Probably the best bait for this fishing is a quarter-inch cube of crust, but maggots are often very effective in heavily fished waters.

It pays to experiment with the length of the link between the cocking shot and bait. Generally speaking the rig works well with its orthodox short link, but there are times when it works better with a 6- or 7-inch trail.

For reasons unknown rudd often feed avidly when the wind is strong and the water choppy. Large bags are sometimes taken in February and March by fishing right into the teeth of the wind with lift tackle. F.J.T. has, on occasions, been tempted to move round the lake until the wind was at his back, but although it made his fishing easier and more comfortable, he has been completely fishless! It is essential to *face the wind* when fishing for late-season rudd.

Undoubtedly there is a connection between the direction of the wind and the feeding behaviour of the fish. Surface food is blown towards one end of the lake and a circulation is set up, which takes the food down towards the bottom. This is where the rudd feed. It is surprisingly easy to keep float tackle out in these conditions. The effect of the circulating water is to pull the tackle into the wind. It seems strange at first, especially as the wind makes it difficult to cast the tackle, but once the float is in position the pull of the circulation overcomes the power of the wind and the tackle remains very stable.

The Windbeater

We regard the windbeater as one of our most useful still-water floats. Certainly its development has allowed us to exploit situations in recent years, which we could not otherwise have dealt with satisfactorily. Although it is called a windbeater, it ought possibly to be referred to as a 'driftbeater', because that is what it really is. It is a stable float, fixed with a bottom-end-only attachment which allows the use of heavier lines; and it registers delicate bites despite the fact that the bait is anchored hard on the bottom. It is the ideal big-fish float because it allows the use of adequate tackle without loss of sensitivity. It is, however, strictly a still-water float. It *can* be used in slow-moving waters, and in its experimental stages we used it to catch roach from the fast flowing River Erne in Ireland. But that was only to test its versatility. There are better floats for such purposes.

The windbeater is comprised of a main body, an unusually long antenna and a buoyant sight-bulb which is one of its most important properties. As its name suggests, the windbeater will cope with rough conditions, but it can only do so if it is set up correctly from the start. It is *not* enough to attach the float, guess the depth and leave it at that! It takes time, patience and imagination to rig the windbeater correctly, but once this has been achieved there is no better float for this particular purpose.

It work best with a line of about 3 lb BS, but, because of its special properties, the large windbeater can be used comfortably with a line of 6 lb.

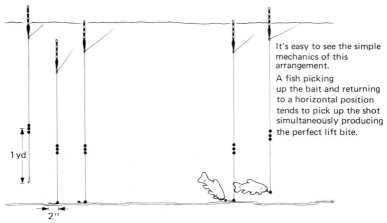

It's easy to see the simple mechanics of this arrangement.

A fish picking up the bait and returning to a horizontal position tends to pick up the shot simultaneously producing the perfect lift bite.

1 yd

2″

(i) How to set up the windbeater rig. Set the float up with as much of the black and white antenna showing as possible by placing bulk shot about three feet from hook.

(ii) Pinch on single large anchor shot about one inch from hook. This shot should be at least heavy enough to sink the rest of the antenna.

(iii) Adjust float so that anchor shot is resting on bottom and sight bob of float is riding on surface.

Figure 40   Windbeater

It can be used as a slider in deep water, but is at its best with a fixed, bottom-end attachment, in water no deeper than the rod's length.

The illustrations show and describe how the shotting should be placed and how the depth setting is finalized. Probably the most significant aspect of the whole procedure is the fact that it is impossible to present the bait anywhere other than on the bottom! The float is over-loaded by the bottom shot and unless that bottom or anchoring shot rests on the bottom, the whole lot will sink! The setting is critical, but essential, and although a number of minor adjustments or shot changes may be necessary to achieve perfection, the time spent in doing so will not be wasted.

After casting, the line is drawn taut to the rod-tip which should be slightly submerged so that drift or wind pressure cannot cause surface drag and pull the float under. The buoyant sight-bulb assists considerably in this respect and remains visible the whole time.

Unlike most other floats, however, the windbeater responds to bites, not by going under the water but by rising out of it! The mechanics of the so-called 'lift' bite are easy to understand if the diagrams are studied.

Very often, after the initial lift, the windbeater will fall flat and glide under slowly as a fish runs off with the bait, but in most circumstances it is not necessary to wait until that stage. There are odd occasions when the lift does not materialize and the sight-bulb simply disappears from sight, but no one, so far, has been able to explain why. Not that it matters!

The extra-long antenna, coupled with the tightline attachment, ensures a stable rig, and a slow, positive bite registration. The whole length of the antenna will rise clear of the water once the bait has been taken and the anchoring shot lifted. The movement appears to be slow and leisurely and this has a remarkably steadying effect upon the angler who has probably waited half an hour or so for his first bite.

The natural reaction to such a bite is not likely to be one of speed and panic; it is more likely to be unhurried and completely confident like the movement of the float itself! The windbeater *dictates* this kind of response and that is one of its great virtues. An angler who waits a long time for a bite from a big fish does not sit poised and ready to strike at the first flicker of the float, but tends to sit back and relax. The slow and unmistakable lift bite produced by the windbeater is ideally suited to his temperament!

The distance at which the windbeater can be fished depends upon the strength of the cross-drift and the diameter of the line being used. Obviously, at long range, the thicker the line the greater the chances of the anchor shot dragging or the sight-bulb submerging. Twenty yards is probably the maximum effective range.

Set correctly, the windbeater cannot fail to register bites from any bottom-feeding fish but, very occasionally, bites will develop that can only be described as too bold, too big or too positive! The antenna rises, topples and the float falls flat at a speed that appears out of keeping with the method of fishing. It often happens at night when the float is illuminated in a torch beam (a situation in which the windbeater really excels) but it also happens in daylight.

Moving the anchor shot an inch or so farther away from the hook (which means, of course, that the float has to be raised by that amount too) will slow the movement down considerably and make the bites much easier to hit.

The Zoomer

A float that has enjoyed a good many seasons of popularity is the zoomer. This float allows you to fish at longer range with light terminal tackle because of the extra weight incorporated in its base. The same light terminal, fished under an orthodox float, would not have anything like the same range. The float itself becomes the casting weight in place of the normal shotting. Indeed very little other weight is necessary.

The dart-like action of the zoomer makes it difficult to cast compared with conventional floats that are weighted with shots on the terminal tackle. Practice is needed to cast it smoothly and accurately, but in one situation the zoomer will catch fish when the regular shotted float will not. This is the hard-fished match water where it is essential to present an ultra-fine and light terminal tackle at long range.

Rudd fishing presents another rather special situation where the zoomer occasionally scores over the conventional float. An angler often has to sit well back in a punt and cast a slow-sinking tackle right to the very edge of marginal rushes. Rudd are easily scared and disappear if the boat is taken in too close.

Zoomers are not much good for deep fishing because they work poorly as sliders and are difficult to cast when fixed at depth, but

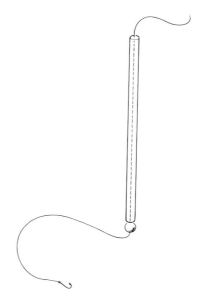

Figure 41   A makeshift
zoomer made by Ken Taylor
for fishing very close to reeds
or rushes. When cast, bait sinks
slowly into position immediately
below loading shot

deep fishing is not needed for rudd. It is sufficient to set the bait
three feet below the float. With no cocking shots necessary, the bait
sinks under its own weight and this is the best medicine to offer rudd
in thick marginal rushes. They'll take it at any point as long as it's
sinking slowly, and a zoomer float allows accurate presentation.

Because the float is self-loaded it leads the bait when it is cast
which is why a lot of casting practice is needed. If you aim at the
base of a rush stem with the float itself, the bait, which tags along
behind, will not end up by becoming attached to the stem! Usually
it lands in the water a yard behind the float and sinks down with a
natural movement to settle immediately underneath the float close
to the rush stems among which the rudd are lurking.

Use of conventionally shotted tackle in such a situation means that
sooner or later you over-cast and the tackle gets snagged. Retrieving
it, or pulling for a break, usually puts paid to the rudd fishing for
some time.

Zoomers are stable floats and very useful for fishing with fine
tackle in a strong wind, but because they are loaded at the base they
have little buoyancy and are virtually useless in a current. *They are
suitable only for use in still or sluggish water.*

The Cocktail

The cocktail, so named because the antenna sections of earlier patterns were made from peacock tail quills, is large and appears at first glance to be somewhat cumbersome, but in fact it is the ideal float for dealing with exceptional situations! Using it in simple and uncomplicated conditions (as is often attempted) is rather like using the proverbial sledgehammer to crack the nut. So much wasted effort!

Everything about the cocktail has a bigger-than-average image, and it could well be regarded as the last remaining link between float fishing and direct ledgering. If the depth and distance are so great that the cocktail cannot cope, all ideas of float fishing might just as well be dispensed with.

It can be used in slow-moving water as a fixed float, and it *can*, in fact, cope with situations just beyond the scope of the largest ducker, but it really scores as a long-range, still-water slider.

Some explanation as to when and where the slider takes over from the fixed float is perhaps necessary at this point, and it can be summed up very briefly. Only two situations call for a sliding float: water a great deal deeper than the rod's length, and a bank situation that, because of obstruction to the rear, calls for an underhand swing or pendulum cast. With the float *and* shotting all concentrated near the hook end of the tackle, casting underhand, or with a sideways swing, is very simple and requires little effort. Some practice is needed to achieve precise accuracy, particularly when the cast is executed sideways, but in most situations a well-loaded cocktail is *an aid* to accurate casting. Its design is such that it will follow a true course and it is a comparatively simple matter to float-fish at 40 yards range in over 10 ft of water. Once in position, the cocktail, rigged as a slider (see diagrams) becomes a very stable float.

The extra-long antenna ensures that the line running from the bottom of the float (towards the rod) is completely sunk and buried well below the surface drift.

The shotting pattern shown is largely self explanatory, but the reason for the bunched bulk shot may be a little obscure. It is done to concentrate the main weight so that it pulls line through the eye of the float up to the stop-knot very positively. After casting, check the line flow momentarily by fingering the reel-spool. Then release it immediately. At this point you will be able to see and feel the line running out through the eye of the float.

The cocktail will work well on a line of 4–5 lb BS, but where long casts are required there is, perhaps, a case for a slightly stronger line to withstand the shock of casting.

There are many waters, particularly man-made reservoirs, where fish such as bream, tench and big roach tend to remain well away from the bank during daylight hours. It is common practice to use a straight ledger tackle to put the bait out at maximum range, but this is often very much a hit and miss affair because there is no visible indication as to where the bait is lying.

A cocktail float tackle cannot be cast as far as a streamlined ledger tackle, but it *can* be put to good use at distances of 40 yards or more;

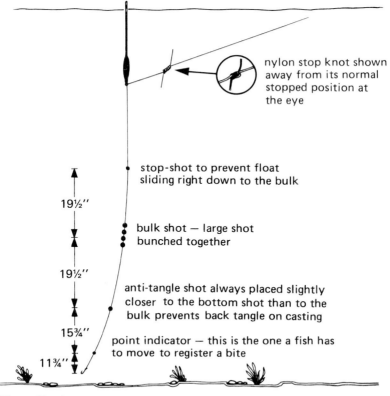

nylon stop knot shown away from its normal stopped position at the eye

stop-shot to prevent float sliding right down to the bulk

19½"

bulk shot — large shot bunched together

19½"

anti-tangle shot always placed slightly closer to the bottom shot than to the bulk prevents back tangle on casting

15¾"

point indicator — this is the one a fish has to move to register a bite

11¾"

Figure 42 Cocktail

and it remains stable and visible at that range. It registers bites that might not be quite so easily noticeable on a direct ledger tackle; but, more important, it also serves as a marker to ensure accurate ground-baiting. With the float in position there is an aiming point at which to throw or catapult groundbait and hookbait samples. The float may not always end up in the groundbaited area, but it is, at least, possible to put groundbait in the hookbait area with each new cast. A straight ledgering situation does not allow such accuracy and this is one of the cocktail's strongest features.

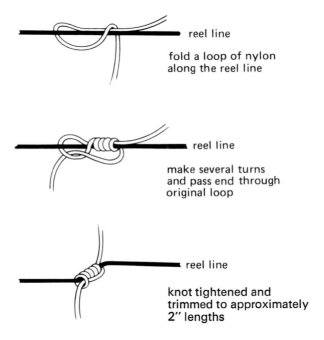

reel line

fold a loop of nylon
along the reel line

reel line

make several turns
and pass end through
original loop

reel line

knot tightened and
trimmed to approximately
2″ lengths

Figure 43 The way to tie a slider knot for a sliding float

We are indebted to Peter Drennan, master float-maker, whose knowledge of float design has been drawn on freely by the authors.

6 Other Methods

Float-ledgering

In the light of modern tackle developments the float-ledger is no longer a very practical rig.

There are, perhaps, a few occasions when it may be necessary to fish a float tackle loaded with a sliding ledger weight. The theory is that the concentrated weight of the ledger holds the bait on the bottom while offering no resistance to a biting fish. What is often forgotten is that the float itself offers resistance! It is not balanced, its buoyancy is not counteracted by intermediate shots and a fish taking the bait has to draw the line through the ledger lead and then pull the float underwater. It doesn't always work that way!

Modern floats, designed as they are to carry shottings capable of dealing with almost every situation, have tended to make float-ledgering unnecessary.

Bottom-loaded floats such as missiles and zoomers may occasionally be useful for long range float-ledgering in still waters. Their buoyancy has been cancelled out by their lead inserts, and it's possible that they could register bites from small fish a long way off, but there are few situations in running water where the float-ledger has an advantage over laying-on, an orthodox ledger or a precisely shotted float tackle.

Paternostering

Except for sea angling, paternoster rigs are no longer in fashion. This is surprising when one considers the advantages of the method. A paternoster provides a means of *anchoring* a bait in midwater or just off the bottom. This can be achieved in two ways:

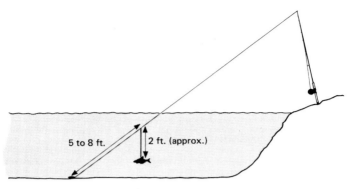

Figure 44

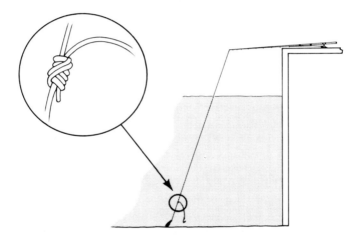

Figure 45

1. By tensioning the line between rod-top and paternoster lead (see *figures 44* and *45*).
2. By using the buoyancy of a float to tension the line between the float and the lead (*figure 46*).

Because it anchors a bait in one position within a limited area, the paternoster keeps the bait 'on view' until that area is visited by a fish, or until a fish that was already in the area starts to feed. One advantage of using a paternoster is that the bait doesn't drift away, so you don't have to keep re-casting or making adjustments for

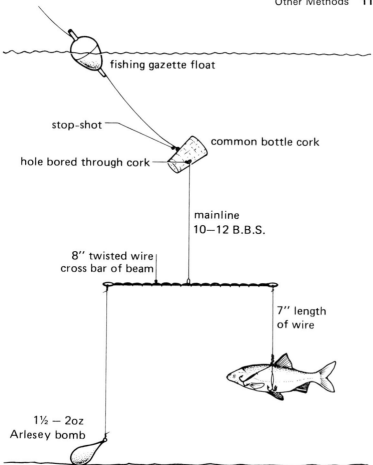

fishing gazette float

stop-shot

common bottle cork

hole bored through cork

mainline
10–12 B.B.S.

8" twisted wire
cross bar of beam

7" length
of wire

1½ – 2oz
Arlesey bomb

Figure 46

variations in depth – unnecessary, because the bait will always fish the same distance off the bottom regardless of depth. As a result of this lack of casting activity the fishing area remains relatively undisturbed.

Because they are anchored, paternoster rigs are particularly suited for coping with windy conditions. In very windy conditions Brown's paternoster is unsurpassed (see *figure 47*).

Paternosters are mainly used for perch, pike and zander fishing – principally because these species are midwater feeders. The paternoster depicted in *figure 45* is particularly suitable for catching bottom-

This 30 lb pike was taken on a roach deadbait fished on the bottom at Wilstone Reservoir, Tring. Captor – Tom Standard of Luton

feeding species of all descriptions – especially where deep water is found close to the bank (i.e. off jetties, etc.) Suspending a bait clear of the bottom is a way of discouraging eels from taking bait intended for other species.

A paternoster rig for windy conditions

The main drawback with most paternoster rigs is that the bait uses the bottom as a sanctuary and, as a consequence, is hidden from fish. Also the rod is necessarily propped high up in the air in order to keep the bait off the bottom. Strong wind makes it difficult to use in this position.

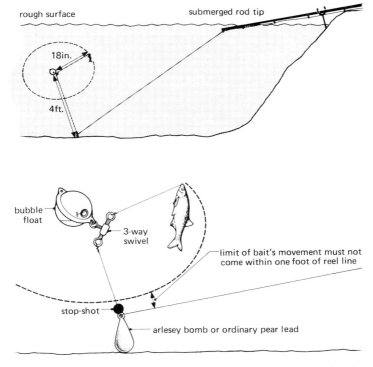

Figure 47   The top drawing depicts Brown's paternoster – notice that the line is completely shielded from the wind. The lower drawing is an enlargement of the terminal tackle. *Note:* the bubble float is *always* attached to the middle eye of the three-way swivel to ensure that the strain of a hooked pike is in line' with the axis of the swivel

A paternoster rig for pike that is effective in strong or even gale-force winds has been designed by Mr Raymond Brown of Coventry. Here is an extract from a letter he wrote after studying F.B.'s book *Pike*:

After reading the section on paternosters I decided to design my own rig for use in gale-force winds or where a strong pull is apparent . . . I *had* to devise a method for fishing a large shallow (i.e. nearly empty) reservoir with thick mud on the bottom, and at *long* range in very rough conditions. The rig proved perfect and we had fish to 18 lb on it from a water (Earlswood Reservoir in the heart of Birmingham) reputed to hold *no* pike.

I used 4 oz sea leads as a last resort to cast my baits into the teeth of a gale. The pike having picked up a bait would run 20–40 yards further before turning the bait. An early strike invariably meant a lost fish when attempted with any one of the classical hook arrangements. In practice once the cast had been made and the line retrieved enough to submerge the bubble float – it (the line that is) was put under an elastic band that stretched around the rod-butt [See p. 143].

There is one drawback; I had one pike run towards me, and striking consisted of a series of pump – strike – pump – strike operations. I think a steady trot backwards (if possible) would be a more acceptable prelude to a strike.

Spinning

The finding of the remains of a cod, together with fish-hooks, on a Neolithic settlement at Hemnor in Denmark, indicates that hook and line fishing was practised some 11,000 years ago. Some time between then and the reign of the Saxon King Edmund (*c.* 870), when the capture of a 30 lb pike on 'a trowling lure of bryte shel' by a Dane in Hickling Broad was recorded, the practice of spinning must have been developed.

Shell seems to have retained its popularity as a material for making artificial lures. When Captain Cook visited Hawaii in the eighteenth century he found the natives using spoon-type shell lures. Even today mother-of-pearl spoons are probably the most attractive of all spinning-baits for perch.

Apart from game fishes, more pike and perch are caught on spinners than any other British freshwater species. Although most other species can and have been taken on spinners, few anglers fish for them in this way.

That perch are sometimes caught by the pike angler and pike by the perch angler indicates an overlap in the techniques used. The most obvious difference in the treatment of these two species is in the size selection of a spoon or spinner. Since perch of over 3 lb are rare, spoonbaits longer than $1\frac{1}{2}$ in are more likely to attract pike. The ideal length for a perch spinner is between $\frac{3}{4}$ in and 1 in.

Swinging-blade or bar-actioned baits like the Mepps Veltex, Vibro and fly-spoon work well, and among plain revolving baits we recommend small Colorados and Devons.

It generally pays to retrieve at a slightly faster rate for perch than for pike, but at times a slow sink-and-draw routine with an un-weighted Mepps is deadly. Indeed, when boat fishing the simple 'pirking' technique used by mackerel and cod fishermen, i.e. sink and draw without line recovery, will take deep-water perch in good numbers.

On the day that F.B. caught this fish on the Stanley beat of the Tay, his first three salmon averaged $22\frac{1}{2}$ lb. He was fishing a bait recom-mended by the ghillies but with the difference that it was four sizes smaller, i.e. $\frac{3}{4}$ oz instead of 1 oz and had a black and brass, rather than the recommended copper and silver, finish. The bait preferred by the ghillies – a 1 oz Toby, produced good results for other members of the party but, with one exception, no big fish.

Although an angler should always try to analyse each fishing experience, in practice his reasons for choosing a particular bait and fishing it in a particular way sometimes defy analysis. F.B. had nothing to go on other than a *strong feeling*. Such a feeling should always be indulged.

Again because of a strong feeling F.B. had deliberately scratched off some of the bait's black enamel before using it and felt that this had contributed to his success – in any event he passed on his scratched bait to the rod who was to fish the beat the next day. The new rod had first the excitement and then the chagrin of hooking, playing and losing the biggest fish of his lifetime.

Of all pike-fishing methods spinning is the most productive. It should be practised in water varying from 2 to 8 ft (which is where most pike live and where most are taken). Many livebait and deadbait pike-fishing specialists believe that only small and medium pike can be taken on spinners. This is not so. Statistics show that more big pike have been taken by spinning than by any other method.

In general terms, a pike spinner is retrieved as slowly as possible.

In order to function properly, however, each type of bait needs to be retrieved at a particular speed. Find out a bait's optimum retrieval speed before putting it into service.

For any given pattern of bait, be it a Norwich spoon or a Canadian bar spoon, there always seems to be an optimum size in terms of achieving its ultimate filling properties. For example, F.B. has frequently caught pike varying in weight from 3 lb into the tens of lbs on $2\frac{1}{2}$ in Colorado spoons. But when he has used a 3 in Colorado (just a half-inch longer) in the hope of fishing more selectively, he has caught nothing.

A spinning line must not only be strong enough to land the expected quarry, it must also accommodate the stresses imposed by continual casting, and, perhaps most of all, the size of hook or hooks that it will have to pull into a pike's jaw. Every angler who does any spinning would do well to ponder this. As a result it is likely that he will either increase his line strength or reduce the size of the trebles carried by the lure.

A quartet of Coventry pike anglers. Left to right: D. Malin, D. Brown,
L. Derricot and R. Brown. By the end of the 1972–3 season they had caught
seventeen pike of over 20 lb. On this occasion they hold fish of 33½ lb, 26 lb
6 oz, 14 lb 12 oz and 25 lb 2 oz

Although all that has been said relates to spinning with artificial
baits, the same arguments apply to spinning with natural baits.

Natural baits should be chosen for their streamlined shape and
'showiness'. For this reason, sprats, dace, bleak and small trout have
always been popular. Eel-tail baits and gudgeon are less showy but
no less successful – and stand up to a great deal of casting.

Trailing

Until recent times, the method of angling known as trailing* was
treated with some contempt. Now, with the advent of echo-sounders,
deep-water thermometers, electric outboards and a greater knowledge of lake biology, including thermal stratification, anglers take a

*Sometimes erroneously called 'trolling'. This latter term literally means 'sink
and draw' a term derived from the German *trollen* 'to draw'.

more enlightened view of trailing. They are beginning to realize that distaste for the method probably derived from an inability to 'see' below the surface of deep lakes in a way that could be revealing and stimulating. But now the nature, climate, and geography of the underwater world can be obtained by the use of echo-sounders and ancillary equipment.

Trailing is, literally, trailing a bait behind a boat. It is of necessity generally aimed at predatory species, but more particularly those that are piscivorous (fish-eating) in character.

One objection to trailing was centred on the technical problem of trailing deep without using tackle so heavy that it ruined the pleasure

Trailing effectively in water deeper than about 12 ft *with ordinary equipment* is very difficult. Letting out more line will not do the trick; going slower stops the bait working attractively; putting heavy weights on the line ruins the pleasure of catching fish as does the use of a lead-cored line. Nevertheless, trailing is the one technique most likely to open up the greatest untapped sporting resources within the British Isles – namely the fish population that lives in the deep parts of our great lochs and lakes of Ireland, Scotland and England

of catching fish. Recently, however, the Americans have perfected leads, paravanes and 'otters' that make any spinner, plug or bait fish at a specified depth – where the fish are known to be shoaling. Furthermore they have invented release devices that free the bait once a fish has struck. This feature allows a fisherman to play his fish without having had to trail with weights or lead-cored lines.

Another notable American advance has been the invention of the electric outboard motor. Thus at one stroke drudgery has been eliminated (perhaps it was the rowing that put most people off trailing) and the sport of trailing has become a quiet, even contemplative, pastime.

F.B. and F.J.T., who have long held a brief for trailing, are of the opinion that it may soon develop into a highly respected branch of the angler's art. F.B. states that the days he has spent trailing on Lough Mask – in a boat equipped with Windermere char-tackle, four-speed electric outboard-motor, echo-sounder and an Admiralty chart – have been some of the most exciting of his fishing career.

Fly-fishing

Lots of articles and at least two books have been written about fly-fishing for coarse fish, yet for various reasons it is practised less nowadays than it was half a century ago.

These reasons include the reluctance of many anglers to purchase fly-fishing equipment and go to the trouble of learning to use it; the very real difficulty of casting with fly tackle on many coarse-fishing waters because of bank obstructions, and a belief by many that it is not quite proper to catch coarse fish on a fly – as exemplified by the prohibition of fly-fishing in match rules, including those for the National Championship matches.

What is not generally realized is that there are some artificial lures that can be fished successfully without the need for a fly rod, flyline or fly reel.

What prompts us to say all this is that we keep catching various kinds of coarse fish on these lures when we are not even trying. At Latimer Park Lakes a short time ago, R.W. hooked a beautiful roach on an imitation midge pupa, a fish estimated at not less than $1\frac{1}{2}$ lb. A day or two later, he caught another of about the same size, on a leaded mayfly nymph from a Test sidestream. He was intrigued by this, so after releasing the fish, he broke off the point and barb of the hook and then tried to see if other roach in the shoal were equally interested. They certainly were; that nymph was taken no less than twenty-six times and if he had wanted to, he reckons he could have caught several dozen, and these were all good-sized fish of a pound or more.

Recently, Pat Russell caught a roach of $1\frac{1}{2}$ lb while grayling-fishing with a leaded shrimp. A few years ago, Peter Thomas had a $2\frac{1}{2}$ lb roach from Hanningfield on a small black lure.

On the Tweed some years ago, Peter Stone, F.J.T. and R.W. caught numbers of good roach on little green nymphs, and F.B. will vouch for the fact that on Loch Lomond, R.W. caught roach after roach, fish of $\frac{3}{4}$ lb to $1\frac{1}{4}$ lb, on a small pheasant-tail nymph.

All these fish were, in fact, caught with fly-fishing tackle, but a combination of a 12 or 13 ft, modern glass match-rod, a fixed-spool reel, and light monofil line can fish these flies just as well, perhaps even better.

The leaded shrimp and the mayfly nymph, leaded, weigh as much as a BB shot, and can be cast a fair distance on a $2\frac{1}{2}$ lb BS line without any additional weight. Other less heavy patterns can be fished perfectly well on the same tackle, simply by pinching enough ordinary split shot on the line. The important thing to remember is that artificial lures need to be fished differently from the usual coarse-fish baits. Whereas trout will often pick up a fly that is lying un-moving on the bottom, coarse fish seldom do so. You have to move the lure (or let the current move it) so that it looks alive – unless, of course, you are using a floating fly which, we must admit, cannot be fished as successfully with coarse-fishing tackle as it can with a fly rod. True, you can try fishing it with a float shotted above and below to lie flat, or with a wooden casting weight that just floats, but in our experience it isn't really all that killing.

Sunk flies, on the other hand, can be very deadly. So far we have mentioned only how good they can be for roach. They can also be extremely effective for rudd, chub and perch. A green nymph with a gold rib can catch rudd after rudd, and big ones too, fished with a swan shot pinched a couple of feet above it, cast out, and retrieved sink-and-draw. And just try the same technique but with a No. 6 Muddler Minnow in a good chub swim – the fish will nearly take the rod out of your hand. In the case of chub, you can search a swim very thoroughly, trying first a light shot loading and working the lure across on a tight line so that it fishes just below the surface. If that doesn't work (and it often does in hot weather) you can increase the shot to the point where you can fish it like a swinging ledger, bumping bottom as the current takes it round.

Some anglers are scared to try this for fear of losing expensive flies, but in practice the losses are not serious. They are less than in conventional fly-fishing because you don't get hung up on your back-cast; and you'd be unusually unlucky to lose so many flies that they cost you as much as a gallon of maggots, even if you used bought flies instead of tying your own, a skill that is very easily acquired.

As for perch, a lure can be at least as deadly as any other thing you could use, not excluding worms, livebait or spinners. Before disease hit the perch at Hanningfield, we would have backed any angler to catch more perch in a day's fishing, using a two-hook tandem lure, than anyone else would by spinning or bait fishing. R.W. has had spells there when he caught a perch over 2 lb every throw, for a dozen successive casts. It was easy at times to catch half a hundred-weight in an hour, if you could find the shoals. It would have been easier still if we had been allowed to fish the same lures on monofil line, long rod, and fixed-spool reel with a couple of swan shot to take them down.

In rivers, you can fish various artificial lures on float tackle, provided there is sufficient current. You use exactly the same rig as for long-trotting, only instead of a baited hook, you tie on an artificial lure, and instead of taking care to trot down with it just off the bottom, or barely dragging, you keep checking the float so that the lure rises in the current. Then you release line to let the float go a couple of feet farther downstream, check it again, and so on till you've reached the full length of your chosen swim. The bites are nearly always very positive indeed, and come a fraction of a second after you've checked the float. Not only does the float dive; quite often your rod-tip is pulled over as well, specially by chub.

There are no records of anyone having caught a barbel in Britain by this method, but they catch barbel regularly on artificial lures in Germany, and we are sure that it could be done here as well.

Very little is known about fishing imitative lures such as shrimps, nymphs, caddis, pupae, plus hairwing and streamer lures, simply because too few anglers will experiment. The increase in the cost of maggots and worms may lead a few more people to try. We hope so. There is a considerable future for artificial lures in coarse fishing, perhaps far beyond anything now visualized.

7 Nothing New in Fishing

An ingenious method

The first swimfeeder?

If you will bait a stream, get some tin boxes made full of holes, no bigger than just fit for a worm to creep through; then fill these boxes with them, and having fastened a plummet to sink them, cast them into the stream with a string tied there to, that you may draw them forth when you list. By the smallness of the holes aforesaid, the worms can crawl out but very leisurely, and as they crawl the fish will resort about them.

Nicholas Cox, *The Gentleman's Recreation* . . . 'Collected from Antient and Modern Authors Forrein and Domestick, Etc.' (1674)

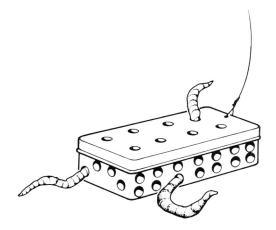

Figure 48

Few anglers realize that most so-called modern fishing tackle and, for that matter, fishing techniques, are only modern in the sense that they represent the latest stage in the development of tackle and methods which have long been in use. An 'inventive' angler would be hard put to prove his claim to have devised something entirely new.

John Waller Hills, in his classic book *A Summer on the Test* (1924), wrote: 'It is perhaps not surprising that I claim no wonderful discoveries. In fact I have made none. What I have learnt, very painfully, has been invented by others.'

To show how seldom something entirely new is created in the field of angling today, we offer some examples of what are often thought to be modern tackles and techniques. They are all nearly as old as the proverbial hills.

Of the two novelties which R.W. can claim to have contributed to the sport of angling, only one – his *balanced crust bait* – is new in the sense that it is not a development of an old concept. His *electric bite-alarm* represents but one more stage in the development of audible bite-indication, a system that started life at least two hundred and fifty years ago with the introduction of the humble rod-bell. The rod-bell, nowadays almost exclusively used by sea anglers, was in earlier times used by freshwater anglers to indicate a bite when they were fishing at ground (ledgering).

By the same token, Leslie Moncrieff's *atomic-lighted bite-indicator*, an essential attachment for bait-fishermen who operate after dark (this glowing device can be fitted to rod-tip, line or float) is but a development of the visual bite-indicator for night fishing described by Robert Howlett in the *Angler's Sure Guide* (1706):

I was lately informed, 'tis a good way to angle for Carps in a dark Night, with such a Rod and Line floated thus, with Glow Worms; Scrape an Inch in length of the Butt End of a large Swan Quill till it be transparent, and prick three or four Holes into it with a small Needle, round the Tip of the Butt-End, to let in Air; then cut off an inch and a half in length of that scraped End, and bind the open end twice or thrice about with a waxed Silk, and fit a cork near half an Inch long to go stiff into it. When you have put a Glow-worm or two into the scraped piece of Quill, stop it with the cork.

When you have a Bite, strike not before your Glow-worm be gone a Little out of sight: and make use of a Lanthorn.

So much for the illuminated float!

Next, that supposedly modern invention the *swing-tip*. This cunning form of bite-indicator was first mentioned in the third edition of *The Angler's Pocket Book: or Compleat English Angler*, published in 1805 (author unknown).

From this unknown author's description of the swing-tip – which he called *The Elastic or New Invented Superficial Float* – F.B. has made this drawing.

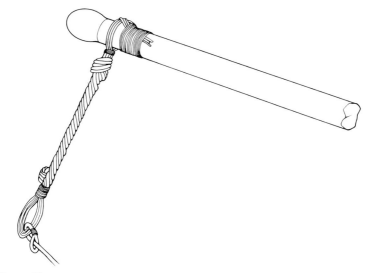

Figure 49

The illustration shows the top of a fixed-line rod. The swing-tip, made with five twisted pig's bristles, is fastened to the rod-top with waxed silk binding. The bristles are looped at the end to receive the line, and the loop is whipped with more silk binding. (The fact that such pig bristles could be found at the start of the nineteenth century reflects the evolution of the domestic pig since that period. Anglers would be hard put to find suitable bristles on the body of a modern pig.)

The *doughbobbin*. A 'modern' invention described perfectly in Robert Venables's book *The Experienc'd Angler: or Angling Improved* (1662). The illustration of an angler using what fishermen have later come to describe as a 'doughbobbin' – since they often use a lump of dough in lieu of a cork – comes from these lines:

Some use to lead their lines heavily, and to set their cork about a foot or more from the end of the rod, with a little lead to buoy it up, and thus in violent swift streams they avoid the offence of a flote, and yet perfectly discern the biting of a fish.

Figure 50

According to William Radcliffe, in *Fishing from the Earliest Times* (1921), all four methods of fishing – spear (harpoon), net, hand-line and rod – were being used by the ancient Egyptians *c.* 2000 BC.

Judging by the height of the angler portrayed in the mural, the rod then in vogue was five or six feet long, and *tapered*. Furthermore, since the fish is being lifted from the water by its mouth, one may assume that the fisherman has not snatched it, but caught it on a baited hook. He is, without doubt, a true angler, the first on record.

The grinner knot

In 1970 one of us (R.W.) invented a new knot for attaching eyed hooks and swivels. As with many inventions, it may be discovered that someone else invented this knot long before 1970, but at present we have seen no earlier record of it.

The *rod*, which you might think a relatively modern invention, was in use
four thousand years ago. The earliest reproduction of angling *c.* 2000 BC.
From P. E. Newberry, *Beni Hasan*

Turn for turn it is stronger than any other knot we know, and has
the advantage of being much more reliable. The end of the line is
trapped by all the turns, so that slipping is impossible. There are two
ways of tying this knot. The end product is the same, but some
anglers find one method easier, some the other. The diagrams show
both methods.

When the grinner knot was described in *Trout and Salmon*, some
readers pointed out that it could be developed so as to join two
strands of line. This development is known as the double grinner
knot. Turn for turn it is stronger than the blood knot, and perhaps
fractionally stronger than the water knot, but superior to the latter
in that it is much neater.

It can be used for joining strands differing in thickness by a much
greater amount than is safe for blood knots, and shares with the
water knot the advantage that its ends are safe to use as droppers or
attachments for paternoster tackles. Blood-knot ends are unreliable
for either purpose.

As with the grinner knot, the ends in a double grinner are trapped
by all the turns of the knot and cannot possibly slip.

After a little practice, most anglers find these grinner knots easier
to tie than blood and half-blood knots; there is no fiddling about,
trying to poke an end between two adjacent strands. Indeed, when
challenged, R.W. tied a grinner knot to the eye of a fly while blind-
folded.

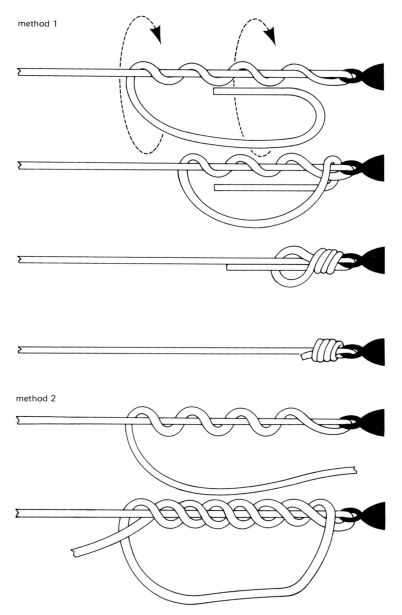

method 1

method 2

Figure 51 Two methods of tying a grinner knot

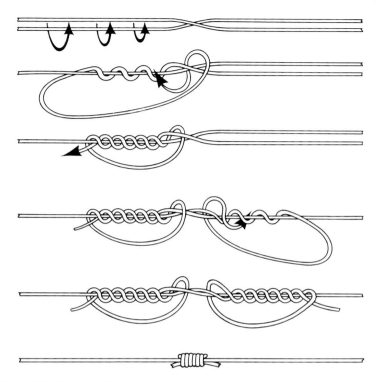

Figure 52   Double grinner knot

The water knot

This little gem of a knot, rediscovered by that fine all-round angler, Arthur Cove, was described by F.B. in a fishing magazine and, later, in his book *Pike* (1971). F.B. and H.F., researching for a book they were writing together in 1972,* traced the history of this knot from author to author back through the centuries to the first book on angling written in English: Dame Juliana Berners's *A Treatyse of Fysshynge wyth an Angle*, first printed in 1496 (as part of *The Boke of St Albans, 2nd edition*) but probably written *c.* 1425.

Among other novelties, the *Treatyse* also described rod joints with ferrules, a hollowed bottom joint to take the top joint, butt-spike

*Falkus and Buller's Freshwater Fishing (Macdonald and Jane's).

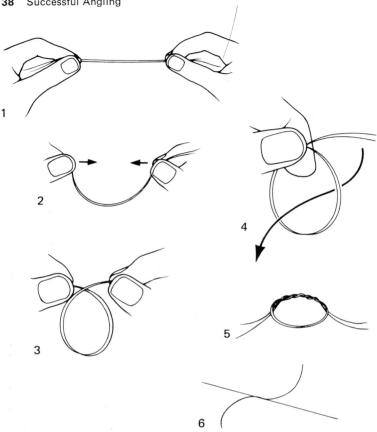

Figure 53   The water knot
– unsurpassed for joining two
lengths of nylon

and spade-end hooks – although these were already thousands of
years old. Spade-ends were 'discovered' by the British angling public
after the Second World War. Previously, what demand there was for
these flatted-end or 'tad' hooks, as the professionals called them,
was a commercial one. Anglers who were brought up on hooks tied
to gut or nylon may be surprised to learn that this supposedly
modern hook is the oldest of all. Spade-end hooks, eyed hooks and
even spade-end eyed hooks have been in use since the Bronze Age.
Five-thousand-year-old hooks found in Crete have flatted forged
ends, pierced for line attachment.

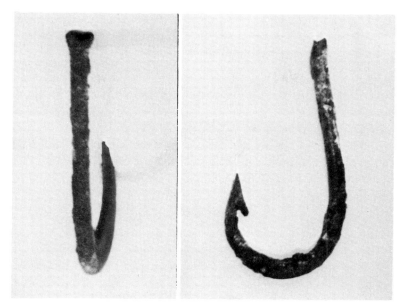

The oldest British hook: a spade-end found in the Thames at Grays, Essex.
Now on view at Colchester Museum. Estimated age: 2500 years

The groundbait marker-buoy

F.B. first described a groundbait marker buoy in *Rigs and Tackles* (1967), and later in *Falkus and Buller's Freshwater Fishing* (1975). It is a simple means of providing a target for groundbait and hookbait where the sheer expanse of lake or reservoir makes it difficult to put both in the immediate vicinity of each other.

F.B. thought that he had been the first to describe the device. He was forestalled by Mrs Hannah Wolley who, three centuries before, wrote in *The Accomplish'd Lady's Delight* (1675):

And that you may always fish in that place where you have cast your ground-bait, you must have a buoy to tye out, and then you art sure to fish right.

F.B. wrote:

I have used the groundbait marker-buoy method with great success. It has enabled me to have fine sport on days when nearby anglers were hard pressed to catch a single fish. Although I developed the method for ledgering, I have also found it a very useful aid to float fishing – particularly at long range.

The consistently successful angler is the man who gives himself the best possible chance of catching a fish during every fishing moment. Part of his repertoire is the judicious use of groundbait – the purpose of which is to attract fish. But this in itself does not guarantee success. To be

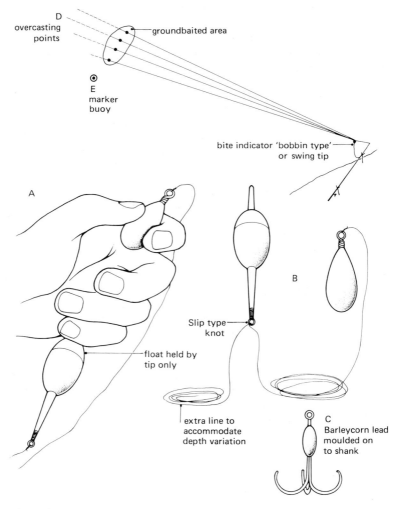

Figure 54

effective, his hookbait *must* fall inside his groundbait area otherwise the groundbait will merely tend to draw fish *away* from the hookbait.

Often, however, after throwing out his groundbait an angler becomes uncertain of its exact position, and can no longer ensure that his hookbait always falls in the right place. This is particularly evident when he is ledgering open sheets of water, such as lakes and reservoirs, which are devoid of local landmarks. In waters such as these, the accurate pinpointing of the groundbaited area is very difficult, and becomes progressively more difficult as the casting range increases.

This difficulty is easily overcome. If the groundbait is placed close to an anchored float acting as a marker-buoy, the subsequent positioning of the hookbait can be judged with complete accuracy.

First, ascertain the depth of water at the place you wish to groundbait. Do this by fitting up a float-fishing outfit consisting of rod, fixed-spool reel, 4 lb BS line, sliding float, and plummet. The sliding float should be of the modern 'Billy Lane' type with a very small eye for the line to run through. Tie a special sliding stop-knot on the line above the float. Set the float at the estimated depth and cast out to the desired area. The depth has been over-estimated if the float lies on its side; under-estimated if it disappears. Adjust the stop-knot until the float just cocks. The distance between float and plummet now indicates the true depth.

From a reserve spool, cut off a length of 6 lb BS nylon which exceeds the measured depth by about two feet. Tie one end to a $2\frac{1}{2}$ oz Arlesey bomb, and the other end to the bottom eye of a medium pike-float. Anchored by the lead, the pike-float will serve as a marker-buoy.

Hold the lead between thumb and forefinger; the top of the float between palm and little finger. Throw the lead so that it pulls the float out behind it. When the float settles (point E in the diagram) its movement is restricted, since it has been allowed only two feet of spare anchor line.

Fit up a swimfeeder ledger rig. Fill the feeder with groundbait and cast slightly beyond and to one side of the marker-buoy. The moment the feeder hits the water, retrieve it to a point level with the float (area F) and allow it to sink. As soon as the feeder touches bottom, give the rod a fierce pull to eject the groundbait. Retrieve, fill up the feeder and repeat the operation. Twenty minutes of this will ensure that a carpet of groundbait is accurately placed in position.

You are now ready to start fishing. And knowing exactly where to place each cast, you can fish with complete confidence.

The swimfeeder remains with the terminal tackle of the ledger rig. Re-bait it fairly frequently during the first few hours of fishing. This will entail more casting than you might normally expect to do, but if carefully performed, this activity will excite the fish rather than frighten them.

Provided that the groundbaited area is within accurate lobbing range, bream fishermen should augment the supply of swimfeeder groundbait with hand-thrown balls of heavier texture groundbaits: e.g. a bread/bran mixture. Bream have huge appetites and require more substantial ground-baiting than other species.

At the end of the day's fishing, retrieve the marker-buoy with a casting drag. The drag can be fashioned from a piece of wire, or from a large treble hook. *Don't* cast directly at the buoy. First walk several paces along the bank either to right or left, then cast across at an angle beyond the buoy. Return to your original position before retrieving, and the drag will catch the anchor line first time.

It is interesting to reflect that in addition to its material advantages, the marker-buoy method of fishing offers a certain spiritual comfort. When lake or reservoir fishing, the angler is easily overwhelmed and dispirited by the great sheet of water which confronts him. With the marker-buoy, a specific fishing area is defined. The angler is no longer casting into a featureless expanse, but concentrating on a piece of water which in his imagination seems intimate and friendly. Far from losing heart, he is made eager by a sense of involvement – for in effect he has created a little 'swim'.

Deadbait ledgering for pike

There are several anglers who claim to have introduced the ledger method of fishing a stationary deadbait and not a few who claim to have been the first to use herrings for this purpose. It was, of course, F.J.T. who rediscovered the method during the 1950s, and it was he who, through his writings, was responsible for its popularity through-out Britain. But once again, both method and bait were first described in the *Treatyse*: Here is the passage, with the spelling modernized:

Take a codling hook, and take a roach or a fresh herring, and a wire with an hole in the end, and put it in at the mouth, and out at the tail, down by the ridge of the fresh herring; and then put the hook in after, and draw the hook into the cheek of the fresh herring; then put a plumb of lead upon your line a yard long from your hook, and a float in midway between; and cast it in a pit where the pike useth, and this is the best and most surest craft of taking the pike.

Casters and chrysalids

Is the 'caster', that darling bait of the match-fisherman, new?

As a modern coarse-fishing bait the caster is almost as popular as the ubiquitous maggot. Many believe that it was introduced after

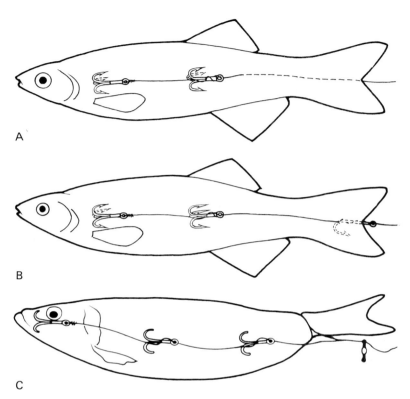

A

B

C

Figure 55 Three ways of attaching a deadbait

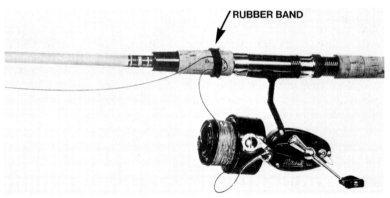

Brown's clever method of 'slip-anchoring' a line under a rubber band could be used in many other situations − including deadbait ledgering

the Second World War by northern and midland match-anglers – much to the chagrin of certain southerners who used the bait between the wars but called it a chrysalis. In fact the bait was described by Captain T. Williamson in *The Complete Angler's Vade-Mecum* (1808).

. . . gentles are very easy to obtain; but they speedily change to chrysalis state, if subjected to much heat. I have several times found my gentles, of but two or three days' growth, changed by being only one day exposed to the warmth of the sun in my basket, to that form, in which, however, they are by no means an unwelcome bait.

Coloured maggots

Neither is the practice of dyeing gentles a new one. It's very old indeed, since it too was described some three hundred years ago by Mrs Hannah Wolley in *The Accomplish'd Lady's Delight*:

If you put some gentles into a box, where vermilion has been, they will live in it two or three days, and will become of a very transparent colour, and keep so in the water when you fish with them.

So we could go on. It may be a disappointment to learn that tackle or methods we *thought* we'd discovered or invented were already in use a century or more ago. But that's of little importance. What *is* important is the understanding and development of those ideas, for it is their proper application to the task in hand that leads to successful angling.

Bibliography

As a complete change from the comprehensive bibliographies usually found at the back of angling instructional books, we thought that it would be interesting for the reader to know our ten *favourite* fishing books. Each of us prepared his list independently. There is a slight overlap in the lists, and it is clear that most of the books were chosen for *pleasure* rather than instruction – books that can be read again and again. Many of the books are out of print (original publication dates are shown), but they are in our opinion worthwhile searching for in libraries and second-hand bookshops.

Richard Walker's list of favourite books
Loved River H. R. Jukes (1935)
Sporting Sketches Francis Francis and A. W. Cooper (1878)
At the Tail of the Weir Patrick A. Chalmers (1932)
An Angler's Hours H. T. Sheringham (1905)
An Open Creel H. T. Sheringham (1910)
Days Stolen for Sport Philip Geen (*c.* 1900–1910)
What I Have Seen While Fishing Philip Geen (1905)
Lines in Pleasant Places William Senior (1920)
A Summer on the Test J. W. Hills (1924)
Rod and Line Arthur Ransome (1929)

Books by Richard Walker
Rod-building for Amateurs (1952; revised edition 1961)
Still-Water Angling (1953; revised edition 1976)
Drop Me A Line with Maurice Ingham (1953)
Walker's Pitch (1959)
No Need to Lie (1964)
Carp Fishing (1960)
How Fish Feed (1960)
Fly Dressing Innovations (1974)

Fred J. Taylor's list of favourite books
Coarse Fishing Sheringham (1912)
Sea Trout Fishing Falkus (1962)
The Angler's Bedside Book Wiggin (1965)
The Art of Coarse Fishing Bazely (1932)
Drop Me A Line Ingham and Walker (1953)
Still-Water Angling Walker (1953)
Confessions of a Carp Fisher 'BB' (1950)
Through the Fish's Eye Sosin and Clark (1973)
Pike Buller (1971)
Freshwater Bass Bergman (1942)

Books by Fred J. Taylor
Angling in Earnest (1958; revised edition 1980)
How to Fish the Upper Great Ouse (1959)

Favourite Swims (1960)
Fish of Rivers, Lakes and Ponds (1961)
Tench booklet (1966)
Fishing Here and There (1968)
Tench (1971)
101 Fishing Trips (1976)
Fishing for Tench (1979)
My Fishing Years (1981)
Reflections on the Water (1982)
Reflections of a Countryman (1982)

Hugh Falkus' list of favourite books
A Man May Fish T. C. Kingsmill Moore (1960)
A Summer on the Test J. W. Hills (1924)
A Treatyse of Fysshynge wyth an Angle attributed to Dame Juliana
   Berners (1496)
Angling Diversions A. Courtney Williams (1945)
Fishing from the Earliest Times William Radcliffe (1921)
Going Fishing Negley Farson (1942)
The Fisherman's Bedside Book compiled by 'BB' (1945)
The Fishes of the British Isles and N.W. Europe Alwyne Wheeler (1969)
The Life of the Sea Trout G. H. Nall (1930)
The Open Sea Two volumes Sir Alister Hardy (1956 and 1959)

Books by Hugh Falkus
Sea Trout Fishing (First Edition) (1962)
The Stolen Years (First Edition) (1965)
Falkus and Buller's Freshwater Fishing (1975)
Sea Trout Fishing (Second Edition) (1975)

Fred Buller's list of favourite books
Fishing from the Earliest Times William Radcliffe (1921)
The Sportsman in Ireland Cosmopolite (1840)
Ancient Angling Authors W. J. Turrell (1910)
Wild Sports of the West Wm. Maxwell (1832)
Fish and Fishing J. J. Manley (1877)
British Freshwater Fishes C. Tate Regan (1911)
A History of Fly Fishing for Trout J. W. Hills (1921)
The Practice of Angling O'Gorman (1845)
The Angler's England Patrick Chalmers (1938)
Notable Angling Literature James Robb (1947)

Books by Fred Buller
Rigs and Tackles (1967)
Pike (1971)
Falkus and Buller's Freshwater Fishing (1975)
The Domesday Book of Mammoth Pike (1979)
Pike and the Pike Angler (1981)

Index

Italic figures refer to captions